D0917640

A Lawyer's Guide to
Dangerous Dog Issues

JOAN SCHAFFNER
EDITOR

TORT TRIAL & INSURANCE PRACTICE SECTION

Defending Liberty
Pursuing Justice

Cover design by ABA Publishing.

The materials contained herein represent the opinions and views of the authors and/or the editors, and should not be construed to be the views or opinions of the law firms or companies with whom such persons are in partnership with, associated with, or employed by the American Bar Association, or the Tort Trial & Insurance Practice Section, unless adopted pursuant to the bylaws of the Association.

Nothing contained in this book is to be considered as the rendering of legal advice, either generally or in connection with any specific issue or case; nor do these materials purport to explain or interpret any specific bond or policy, or any provisions thereof, issued by any particular franchise company, or to render franchise or other professional advice. Readers are responsible for obtaining advice from their own lawyers or other professionals. This book and any forms and agreements herein are intended for educational and informational purposes only.

© 2009 American Bar Association. All rights reserved.

No part of this publication may be reproduced, stored in a retrieval system, or transmitted in any form or by any means, electronic, mechanical, photocopying, recording, or otherwise, without the prior written permission of the publisher. For permission, contact the ABA Copyrights & Contracts Department at copyright@abanet.org or via fax at 312-988-6030.

Printed in the United States of America.
13 12 11 10   5 4 3 2

Library of Congress Cataloging-in-Publication Data

Catalog-in-Publication data is on file with the Library of Congress.
A Lawyer's Guide to Dangerous Dog Issues
Joan E. Schaffner, editor
ISBN: 978-1-60442-552-9

Discounts are available for books ordered in bulk. Special consideration is given to state bars, CLE programs, and other bar-related organizations. Inquire at Book Publishing, ABA Publishing, American Bar Association, 321 North Clark Street, Chicago, Illinois 60654-7598.

www.ababooks.org

Contents

Acknowledgments vii

About the Authors ix

Foreword xv

Chapter 1

Introduction. 1

PART I

Dangerous Dog Laws 5

Chapter 2

Ordinances Targeting Reckless Owners and Damaged Dogs:

Is Canine Profiling Effective?. 7

What Is a Pit Bull?. 8

Werewolf, Lassie, or Just Plain Dog? 8

The "CSI" Effect: Doggy DNA and Its Impact

on Breed-Discriminatory Laws 12

Liability Questions 13

What Do the Studies Show: Are Canine-Profiling Laws Effective?. . . 15

The Other End of the Leash: A New Breed of Law Targeting

Reckless Owners 18

Restricting Dog Ownership by Certain High-Risk Persons 18

Taking a Community-Policing Approach to Reckless Owners

and Dangerous Dogs. 20

Restricting Tethering and Chaining. 21

Pack Mentality 22

Requiring DNA of Deemed Dangerous Dogs 22

Protecting the Public While Preserving Responsible

Owners' Property Rights. 23

Chapter 3
The Constitutionality of Breed-Specific Legislation:
A Summary. 25
Breed Discrimination: Breed-Specific Legislation 26
Tellings v. Toledo: A Rational Case Reversed 27
  Judicial Review 28
  Void for Vagueness. 29
  Procedural Due Process 30
  Equal Protection and Substantive Due Process 31
  Privileges and Immunities; Takings. 33
Challenging BSL 34
  Vagueness. 34
  Procedural Due Process 34
  Equal Protection and Substantive Due Process 35
  Privileges and Immunities; Takings. 35
In Conclusion: A Rational Concurrence 36

PART II
Enforcing and Defending Dangerous Dog Laws. 37

Chapter 4
Prosecuting Dangerous Dog Cases 39
Culpability of Owners 39
Witnesses for the Prosecution 41
  Victim 41
  Animal Control or Police Officer 42
  Neighbors and Other Witnesses 43
  Forensic Nurses. 43
  Treating Physicians 44
  Veterinarian or State Veterinarian 44
  Animal Behaviorist 45
  DNA Expert. 45
Conclusion 45

Appendix 4–1
Virginia's Dangerous Dog Law 47

Appendix 4–2
Virginia's Dangerous Dog Registry 55
   City of Richmond: Dangerous Dog # 0641 55
   City of Newport News: Dangerous Dog # Unassigned 56
   City of Newport News: Dangerous Dog # 0876 57
   York County: Dangerous Dog # 0566 58

Chapter 5
Defending Allegedly Dangerous Dogs: The Florida Experience . . . 61
Introduction 61
Due Process 63
   Substantive Due Process and the Curious Case of Cody. 63
   Procedural Due Process for Liner 66
Defending a Dog at a Dangerous Dog Hearing 68
   Cross-Examination of the Animal Control Officer(s) 69
   Direct Testimony of Dog's Owner 69
   Expert Testimony. 70
Conclusion 70

PART III
Breed Discrimination in the Private Sector 73

Chapter 6
**Hounded by Homeowner Associations and Dogged by Zoning
Boards: Litigating Breed-Specific Restrictions** 75
The Recent Rise of Community Associations
and Restrictive-Covenant Governance 75
The Rise of Breed-Specific and Pet-Specific Restrictive Covenants . . . 77
   Covenants and Ordinances Restricting Livestock and Specific Pets 77
   Breed-Specific Dangerous Dog Restrictions. 77

Traditional Rules Governing the Drafting, Interpretation,
and Enforcement of Restrictive Covenants 78
Affirmative Defenses to Breed-Specific and Pet-Specific
Restrictive-Covenant Enforcement Actions 80
   Public Policy Issues—Statutory Restrictions 81
   Statute of Limitations Defenses. 82
   Contractual Ambiguity as an Affirmative Defense 84

Chapter 7
Homeowners Insurance and Dog Ownership: A Primer 87

Introduction 87
Breed Discrimination: Practice and Purported Justifications 88
The Scientific Evidence 90
The Values of Pets and Homeownership 92
A Legal and Policy Response to Breed Discrimination 93
Conclusion 95

Index 97

Acknowledgments

On December 1, 2007, the American Bar Association's Tort Trial & Insurance Practice Section Animal Law Committee sponsored a regional conference entitled "Prosecuting Reckless Owners and Muzzling Dangerous Dogs: Common Sense Solutions for Politicians and Practitioners," at New York University Law School in New York City. The program was co-sponsored by the Animal Farm Foundation and the New York University Student Animal Legal Defense Fund. The conference brought together leaders in the areas of animal welfare with experience in dangerous dog issues to explore the problems associated with breed-specific discriminatory laws—a/k/a breed-specific laws (BSL)—and effective ways to address reckless owners and their dogs. The program included a series of presentations sharing invaluable information with attendees that is compiled here to promote more effective handling of dangerous dog issues nationally. The presenters agreed to become authors and expand and update their materials for inclusion in this publication to provide this information to all.

The author of each chapter is individually noted. Editor Joan Schaffner wishes to thank each of the presenters for their willingness to memorialize in writing their outstanding presentations from the conference: Bernard Rollin, Larry Cunningham, David Furlow, Marcy LaHart, Ledy VanKavage, and Michelle Welch. Brief biographies of each author are included. Moreover, the ABA publication staff, especially Rick Paszkiet, have been very helpful and supportive in the compilation of this book.

About the Authors

Larry Cunningham is an Assistant Professor of Legal Writing at St. John's University School of Law, where he teaches legal writing and legal research. He was formerly an Assistant District Attorney in the Bronx County District Attorney's Office. As a member of the office's Appeals Bureau, he litigated postconviction matters in state and federal court. He was also the Mental Health Coordinator, supervising approximately 15 lawyers who, on a part-time basis, litigated postadjudication insanity review proceedings. Prior to joining the Bronx County District Attorney's Office in 2006, he was a law professor for three years at Texas Tech University, where he taught criminal justice-related courses and directed a criminal litigation clinic. During that time, he was pro bono counsel in a successful, high-profile appeal challenging the prosecution of pregnant women for delivering controlled substances to their fetuses. He was also a visiting professor at Texas Wesleyan University School of Law and Stetson University College of Law.

Cunningham was previously an Assistant Commonwealth's Attorney for the City of Alexandria, Virginia, where he prosecuted juvenile delinquency offenses and gang cases. He holds a B.S. in criminal justice from John Jay College of Criminal Justice, where he was valedictorian, and a J.D. magna cum laude from Georgetown University Law Center, where he was elected to the Order of the Coif and served as an executive editor of the law review. After graduating from Georgetown, he clerked for the Honorable Claude M. Hilton, then-Chief Judge of the U.S. District Court for the Eastern District of Virginia. He is a published author of several law review articles in the areas of juvenile justice, prosecutorial ethics, insurance law, professional responsibility, and criminal procedure.

David A. Furlow is a senior partner at Thompson & Knight. Furlow employs his experience as a former prosecutor and civil attorney to represent clients in trial and on appeal, including insurance defense and coverage, oil and gas, restrictive covenants, and general commercial litigation.

Furlow has broad expertise in First Amendment and Civil Rights Act cases involving the rights of individuals and business owners and has served as Chair of the American Bar Association Tort Trial & Insurance Practice Section's Media, Defamation & Privacy Law Committee. He brings a keen knowledge of history to his work, has appeared in a History Channel documentary, and participates in historical research and writing. On October 7, 2008, he presented oral argument on behalf of the individual, court-appointed executrix Kari Kennedy, in the United States Supreme Court in *Kari Kennedy, Petitioner v. Plan Administrator of DuPont Savings & Investment Plan and DuPont Corporation, Respondents*.

Furlow graduated from the University of Texas School of Law with honors and received a B.A. summa cum laude from the University of Texas at Austin. Furlow's extensive list of law-review articles and Continuing Legal Education presentations are listed on his biography page on the Thompson & Knight LLP Houston website. Homeowner association presentations include "Homeowner Association Wars," Houston Bar Association CLE, May 2003; and "Enforcement of Private Land Use Restrictions: Point-Counter Point—Homeowner's Counter-Argument, That Property and Constitutional Rights Do Not End at the Gates of a Deed-Restricted Community," 22nd Annual Advanced Real Estate Law Course, State Bar of Texas, June 2000.

Marcy LaHart, Esq. in an attorney in solo practice in West Palm Beach, Florida, specializing in public interest environmental law, animal law, and administrative law. She graduated from the University of Florida in 1989, and received her J.D. and certificates in natural resources law and ocean and coastal law from the University of Oregon School of Law in May of 1992. She received the Public Interest Advocate of the Year award from the Environmental and Land Use Section of the Florida Bar in 2003 and has been named an "Animal Hero" for her legal work on behalf of neglected animals for Marathon, Florida's "Stand Up For Animals."

LaHart teaches an animal law workshop as an adjunct faculty member of the University of Miami School of Law. In addition to her environmental cases, LaHart is one of a handful of lawyers in the country devoting a significant portion of their practice to representing people in legal issues regarding their companion animals, including custody disputes, dangerous dog classifications, veterinary malpractice, and pet lemon law issues. Her clients include private citizens, environmental groups, and animal welfare organizations

Bernard E. Rollin (B.A. CCNY, Ph.D. Columbia) is University Distinguished Professor, Professor of Philosophy, Professor of Biomedical Sciences, Professor of Animal Sciences, and University Bioethicist at Colorado State University.

Rollin taught the first course ever done in the world in veterinary medical ethics, which has been a required part of the veterinary curriculum at CSU since 1978, and was a pioneer in reforming animal use in surgery teaching and laboratory exercises in veterinary colleges. He is a principal architect of 1985 federal legislation dealing with the welfare of experimental animals, and has testified before Congress on animal experimentation. He has consulted for various agencies of the governments of the United States and other nations, and currently serves on the Pew National Commission on Industrial Farm Animal Production (PCIFAP) and on the Institute for Laboratory Animal Resources (ILAR) Council of the National Academy of Sciences.

Rollin has lectured extensively (over 1,000 times) on animal ethics, genetic engineering, animal pain, animal research, animal agriculture, veterinary ethics and other topics in bioethics and philosophy to audiences of medical researchers, attorneys, psychologists, philosophers, veterinarians, animal advocates, ranchers, farmers, government officials, students and lay people in the United States and worldwide. He has addressed over 20,000 ranchers and farmers on animal rights and animal agriculture in forums ranging from the Houston Livestock show to local extension meetings, and has worked with animal scientists and ranchers on alternatives to castration and branding and other issues. He is also founder of the Guide Dogs for the Blind animal care and use committee, and is a member of ACUC for the Centers for Disease Control (Fort Collins).

Rollin has received many prestigious awards from veterinary colleges and associations, animal welfare foundations, and universities, including the Humane Award from the American Veterinary Medical Association in 2007 and the Colorado Agricultural Industry Partner award in 2008. Since 1990, he has written a popular monthly column on veterinary ethics for the *Canadian Veterinary Journal*. He is the author of over 400 papers and 14 books, of which the best known is *Animal Rights and Human Morality*, which won an Outstanding Book of the Year Award from the American Association of University Libraries and is entering its third edition. His latest books are *Science and Ethics* (Cambridge University Press, 2006) and *Harley Davidson and Philosophy* (Open Court, 2006).

Joan E. Schaffner is an Associate Professor of Law at the George Washington University Law School. She received her B.S. in mechanical engineering and J.D. from the University of Southern California and her M.S. in mechanical engineering from the Massachusetts Institute of Technology. She worked at the law firm of Irell & Manella in Los Angeles California and clerked for the Honorable Marianna Pfaelzer in the Central District of California before coming to GW.

Professor Schaffner teaches Civil Procedure, Remedies, Sexuality and the Law, and Animal Law Lawyering and writes in these areas as well. She is the faculty advisor to Lambda Law, the GLBT student organization at GW, and is faculty advisor and editor-in-chief of the *American Intellectual Property Law Association Quarterly Journal*.

Professor Schaffner directs the GW Animal Law Program, which consists of the GW Animal Welfare Project (AWP), a pro bono effort of faculty and students devoted to researching and improving animal welfare laws in the District of Columbia; seminars in animal law; and a student chapter of the Animal Legal Defense Fund (SALDF). Professor Schaffner codirects the Animal Welfare Project and is the faculty advisor to SALDF. Additionally, Professor Schaffner has testified on behalf of non-breed-specific dangerous dog laws and has presented on animal law panels at conferences worldwide. She is active in various organizations, including as Chair-Elect, Publications Chair, and Editor of the newsletter of the American Bar Association's Tort Trial & Insurance Practice Section Animal Law Committee, Founding Chair of the AALS Section on Animal Law, consumer member for the District of Columbia Board of Veterinary Medicine, and Fellow of the Oxford Centre for Animal Ethics.

Professor Schaffner is a volunteer for Washington Humane Society, fosters feline families, and is committed to saving the lives of homeless animals. She lives with many felines; Jackie, a Jack Russell; and Rocky, a brilliant African Grey parrot.

Ledy VanKavage is the Senior Legislative Analyst for Best Friends Animal Society located in Kanab, Utah. She began her legal career as a judicial law clerk for the Illinois Appellate Court and the U.S. District Court for the Southern District of Illinois. After working at a St. Louis environmental law firm, Green, Hennings, and Henry, she served as an attorney advisor for the U.S. Health and Human Services. VanKavage joined the ASPCA in 1999 and worked there lobbying on behalf of animals as the Sr. Director of Legislation and Legal Training, spearheading the passage of twenty animal welfare bills in the Illinois legislature.

VanKavage has worked extensively in the humane movement. In 1985 she organized the Madison County Coalition Against Pound Seizure, successfully stopping the sale of animals for research from her county animal control facility. She then founded the Madison County Humane Society and served as its president for eight years. In 1992 she cofounded the Illinois Federation of Humane Societies and served on its board for ten years. She was also a cofounder of Operation SPOT (Stop Pet Overpopulation Today) in the St. Louis Metropolitan area and served as a board member for eight years. She is a Vice-Chair of the American Bar Association's Tort Trial & Insurance Practice Section Animal Law Committee, and Former Chair of the Animal Law Committee's Dangerous Dog Subcommittee. VanKavage also serves on the Animal Farm Foundation Board. She has been interviewed on the subject of dangerous dog issues by the *New York Times*, MSNBC, NPR's *Justice Talking*, the *Chicago Tribune*, and the *St. Louis Post Dispatch*.

VanKavage graduated from Eastern Illinois University with a B.S. in zoology and attended graduate school at Southern Illinois University at Edwardsville in environmental studies before earning her J.D. at St. Louis University. VanKavage currently resides in Collinsville, Illinois, where she and her husband have adopted three brindle pit bulls, Goodall, Che, and Bella, and also oversee a feral cat colony in the neighborhood.

Michelle Welch is an Assistant Attorney General in the Virginia Attorney General's Office where she handles all animal law questions for the Office. She is frequently an advisor to localities on animal cruelty and dogfighting prosecutions and has served as a special prosecutor on these cases. She also handles Sexually Violent Predator Commitments and represents the Virginia Department of Alcohol Beverage Control.

Welch was formerly a Deputy Commonwealth's Attorney for the City of Richmond, where she was the Animal Abuse Prosecutor and handled all the animal-related cases for that office. She has lobbied legislators, convincing them to pass a law preventing convicted animal abusers from owning animals. Moreover, through her efforts, the Virginia AG's office played a critical role in amending the animal fighting laws in Virginia in 2008 such that Virginia now has one of the best animal fighting laws in the nation. In fact, the office was honored by the Humane Society of the United States with the Humane Law Enforcement Award in 2008. Through her national reputation on animal law, her passion, and endurance, she has elevated the issue of animal fighting and cruelty to the public conscience and has brought the Virginia AG's office to the forefront of regional efforts to end cruelty against animals.

Additionally, Welch is an educator. She is sought out as an expert in the field of animal law by groups around the state and on the national level. She has taught all of the general district judges in Virginia on the subject and is a regular speaker at the Virginia Animal Control Conference and at animal conferences in Virginia and throughout the nation. Welch also teaches Animal Law as an adjunct professor at the University of Richmond Law School and is an adjunct professor in the Criminal Justice Department at Virginia Commonwealth University. She is Vice Chair of the American Bar Association's Tort Trial & Insurance Practice Section Animal Law Committee and serves as a co-chair of the Animal Litigation Subcommittee.

Foreword

Ethics and Breed-
Discriminatory Legislation

BERNARD E. ROLLIN

By way of orientation: This foreword is not intended to assault the reader with a barrage of facts showing that breed-specific legislation is ill-conceived, though it would not be hard to adduce such facts. For example, there are four times more people killed by lightning per year (100) and five times more people killed by falling coconuts (150) or by hot tap water (150 in Japan alone) than by dog bites (24 per year). Death by bug bite (54 per year) is over two times more likely than death by dog bite; and death by virtue of being struck by a cow (65 per year) is almost three times more likely than death by dog bite.

Since I am a philosopher, the chapter is conceptual. If you affirm that it is both raining and not raining, I don't need to gather weather data to prove you wrong, since the statement is a logical contradiction. Similarly, if I can show that there is a moral conceptual flaw underlying breed-specific legislation, then I don't need to assemble supporting facts. That is what I propose to do.

In the mid-1970s, I began to articulate the moral basis for emerging social ethical concern for animals, for it was clear to any student of Western societies that these cultures were growing ever-increasingly troubled by the treatment of animals, be they research animals, farm animals, zoo animals, or wildlife.

By and large it appeared to me that people were not so much opposed to the standard uses of animals, such as research or animal food production, but rather wanted such use to reflect concern for proper treatment of the animals. It was also clear to me that in *no social use of animals were they getting the best treatment possible consonant with that use.* Thus it seemed obvious to me that society would demand improvements in all areas of animal use. But the question remained— how to articulate this in ethical terms?

At that time, the only extant moral principle embodied in the law, i.e., in our articulated social ethic, was the prohibition against deliberate, sadistic, willful, deviant *cruelty* or outrageous neglect such as not feeding or watering. These laws were in large part based in the Thomistic insight that people who perpetrate such behavior on animals will "graduate" to abusing people, an insight confirmed by decades of research. Even more unsettling, the vast majority of animals suffering, e.g., in agriculture or research, was invisible to the cruelty ethic laws— these laws specifically disavow concern with such areas "ministering to the necessities of man," as one judge put it.

My approach to articulating a stronger ethic for animals was derived from Plato's insight that, when dealing with ethics and adults, one could not teach, one needed to remind, i.e., draw on peoples' extant moral principles, or in my metaphor, use judo not sumo. I reasoned that, if society wished to raise the moral status of animals, it would draw upon extant moral principles for people that the society accepted, appropriately modified, to conceptualize ideal animal treatment. Society has indeed taken elements of the moral categories it uses for assessing the treatment of people and is in the process of modifying these concepts to make them appropriate for dealing with historically unprecedented issues in the treatment of animals, especially their use in science and confinement agriculture.

What aspect of our ethic for people is being so extended? One that is applicable to animal use is the fundamental problem of weighing the interests of the individual against those of the general public. Different societies have provided different answers to this problem. Totalitarian societies opt to devote little concern to the individual, favoring instead the state or whatever their version of the general welfare may be. At the other extreme, anarchical groups, such as communes, give primacy to the individual and very little concern to the group—hence they tend to enjoy only transient existence. In our society, however, a balance is struck. Although most of our decisions are made to the benefit of the general welfare, fences are built around individuals to protect their fundamental interests from being sacrificed for the majority. Thus we protect individuals from being silenced even if the majority disapproves of what they say; we protect individuals from having their property seized without recompense even if such seizure benefits the general welfare; we protect individuals from torture even if they have planted a bomb in an elementary school and refuse to divulge its location. We protect those interests of the individual that we consider essential to being human, to human nature, from being submerged, even by the common good. Those moral/legal fences that so protect the individual human are called *rights* and are based on plausible assumptions regarding what is essential to being human.

It is this notion to which society in general is looking in order to generate the new moral notions necessary to talk about the treatment of animals in today's world, where cruelty is not the major problem, but where such laudable, general human welfare goals, as increasing efficiency, productivity, knowledge, medical progress, and product safety, are responsible for the vast majority of animal suffering. People in society are seeking to "build fences" around animals to protect the animals and their interests and natures from being totally submerged for the sake of the general welfare and are trying to accomplish this goal by going to the legislature.

Animals have natures of their own and biological and psychological interests and needs that flow from these natures, and the thwarting of these interests *matters* to animals as much as the thwarting of speech matters to humans. The agenda is not, for mainstream society, making animals "equal" to people. Rather, it is preserving the common-sense insight that "fish gotta swim and birds gotta fly," and suffer if they do not.

Constitutional rights for animals are, of course, legally impossible, given the legal status of animals as property, the changing of which would require a constitutional amendment, since it is a principle of law that property cannot have rights. But the same functional goal can be accomplished by restricting how animal property can be used. This explains the proliferation of laws pertaining to animals as an effort to ensure their welfare. In 2004 over 2,100 bills devoted to animal welfare were floated at the state level. And this is precisely a major focus of the burgeoning field of animal law, taught in 95-plus law schools.

II

A critical point here is that the new ethic is to be applied to individual animals—they are the moral objects of concern. We need to consider their interests in our use, not merely our ends. And the logic of our consensus social ethic for humans, as we saw, is the moral guiding principle, being applied to animals.

We now reach a pivotal point in our argument. If we attend to the path our social ethic for humans has taken, it is clear and obvious that the trajectory has been towards ever-increasing concern for individuals qua individuals rather than qua members of a group. It is almost cliché that the original bearers of rights under the U.S. ethico-political system were white, adult, native-born, male, property owners. In other words, group membership counted more than the individual qualities of an individual. The historical evolution of our societal ethic is aptly described as eliminating group designators in our moral treatment and focusing more on individuals. Hence the gradual enfranchisement of black people, immigrants, women, children, and so on. And, as we all know, the task is far from being complete—it took 200 years for us to even begin to live up to our creed that "all men are created equal."

We as a society are beating our breasts about our history of exclusion of certain human individuals from moral concern, so much so that we refuse to utilize group membership even in morally relevant ways. The society has spoken unequivocally against "racial profiling." Any joke based on the group membership of individuals is verboten. Political correctness is rife. And from the perspective of our history, perhaps that is the right thing to do.

The point, however, relevant to our discussion, is that we are not following this logic with regard to our canine companions, which are widely seen by the vast majority of companion animal owners as "members of the family." (The exact percentage of people who so view their animals differs from study to study, but it is at least 70 percent.)

The moral problem in breed-specific bans—be it pit bulls, Rott-weilers, Dobermans, or whatever happens to be the vicious dog of the month—was well encapsulated by the late Franklin Loew, dean of both the Tufts and Cornell Veterinary Schools, when he categorized such laws as "canine racism." This is in fact literally true, since, biologically, breeds of dogs are *races*. And if one is of the postmodernist mind to deconstruct the concept of race as meaningless, the issue is mooted, since there are then no breeds to ban! We shall shortly see that "pit bull" is far more amorphous than a breed.

What some such laws are saying, unequivocally, is that any dog that falls into the group in question is deserving of being singled out, extirpated from family, and euthanized simply by virtue of member-ship in that group. Even if the dog is ten years old, and for ten years has cavorted lovingly with family, friends, and strangers, it deserves to die because it belongs to the group deemed to be incorrigibly evil. In other words, the animal's behavior, personality, and history are deemed irrelevant; the only moral consideration is its breed. Truly this is a resurgence of the very wrong-headed moral thinking we are striving to overcome!

In sum, then, the creation of breed-specific legislation aimed at certain types of animals is incompatible with the thrust of social eth-ics towards including individual animals in the moral circle, as well as with the dominant 20th-century moral theory of judging beings in the scope of moral concern as individuals.

The following question may arise: In cases like exotic Newcastle's disease in poultry, or foot-and-mouth in cattle, we do indeed extermi-nate large numbers of animals that may not be infected. Why then, on epidemiological grounds, not extirpate dangerous dogs in the same preventative fashion? The answer is, first of all, that cattle or chickens in the above case carry a known pathogen that can infect all animals of that sort—hence the slaughter of the entire British cattle herd, because we did not know which animals were affected. If one argues that some dogs are similarly dangerous because some will bite, one would be obliged to exterminate all dogs, because there is no known pathogen or gene leading to violence. If one assumes that all pit bulls are danger-ous, as some jurisdictions do currently, that logically presupposes that there is an identifiable trait of pit-bullness which we shall shortly argue does not exist.

Let us also bear in mind that viciousness is not analogous to harboring a pathogen. Pathogen infection is always deleterious—no one deliberately creates an animal harboring foot-and-mouth disease except for research or terrorist reasons. Aggression in dogs, on the other hand, is sometimes desirable, as in police dogs, sentry dogs, and guard dogs. Furthermore, humans create or elicit aggression in dogs for specific purposes. Most "vicious" dogs are dogs in which aggression has been elicited by owners for socially unacceptable purposes. If this is the case, the culpability for aggression lies with the owner, not the dog, and the owner should be sanctioned. And if such a dog demonstrably has been created, and has hurt people or animals, I have no problem with seizure of such a dog, even though the dog is not in itself culpable. There is an analogy here with criminals who were badly treated as children. Though we (somewhat) understand the causal chain leading to their behavior, we still punish them.

III

The preceding discussion is not the only attack that can be launched against targeting certain breeds. There is also a significant argument from human ethics. This is the argument we alluded to earlier regarding the importance of pets to humans. Anyone who doubted the oft-repeated claims that dogs (especially) and cats are perceived as members of the family in today's society, and who has not seen the research from veterinary schools confirming this, can surely not deny the evidence emerging from the furor surrounding the pet-food poisonings, or the people who refused to be rescued during Hurricane Katrina if they couldn't take their pets with them. In essence, people risked their lives for their pets.

The rise of a bond between humans and such animals rooted not only in mutual symbiotic benefit, but also in something putatively more solid, did not occur until the 20th century with companion animals and the new sort of relationship we formed with them. While humans have enjoyed symbiotic relationships with dogs and, to a lesser extent, with cats for some 50,000 years, the bond was one largely of mutual practical benefit.

In the past 50 or so years, however, dogs (and to a lesser extent, cats and other species) have become valued not only for the pragmatic, economically quantifiable purposes just detailed, but for deep emotional reasons as well. These animals are viewed as members of the family, as friends, as "givers and receivers of love" as one judge put it; and the bond based in pragmatic symbiosis has turned into a bond based in love. This new basis for the bond imposes higher expectations on those party to such a bond on the analogy of how we feel we should relate to humans we are bound to by love and family. A love-based bond imposes a higher and more stringent set of moral obligations than does one based solely in mutual pragmatic benefit.

Humans need love, companionship, emotional support, and to be needed. In such a world, a companion animal can be one's psychic and spiritual salvation. Divorce lawyers repeatedly tell me that custody of the dog can be a greater source of conflict in a divorce than is custody of the children! An animal is someone to hug, and hug you back; someone to play with, to laugh with; to exercise with; to walk with; to share beautiful days; to cry with.

But a dog is more than that. In New York, and other big, cold, tough cities, it is a social lubricant. One does not talk to strangers in cities, unless he or she—or preferably both of you—are walking a dog. Then the barriers crumble.

For more old people than I care to recall, the dog (or cat) was a reason to get up in the morning, to go out, to bundle up and go to the park ("Fluffy misses her friends, you know!"), to shop, to fuss, to feel responsible for a life, and needed.

Our pets have become sources of friendship and company for the old and the lonely, vehicles for penetrating the frightful shell surrounding a disturbed child, beings that provide the comfort of touch even to the most asocial person, and inexhaustible sources of pure, unqualified love.

The phenomenon just described forms the basis for an argument based in human-centered ethical consideration. Are we as a society going to accept—even endorse—laws that cavalierly can rip an object of love and attention—sometimes the only such object for an old person or a street person—from their bosom without their having done anything wrong, merely because they belong to a certain arbitrarily determined class? The mental and physical effects on people bonded to those animals can be catastrophic—that is the reason that some progressive hospitals allow sick people to keep their animals with them in the hospital. What does such an action teach children about ethics, authority and responsibility, when their beloved animal can be taken from them for no valid reason? Such actions fly in the face of common sense and common decency!

IV

Thus far we have argued that breed-specific legislation violates emerging animal ethics by focusing on group membership rather than individual traits and extirpating animals that have not shown themselves to be dangerous, thereby undercutting any analogy with disease control. We have argued that such legislation also hurts humans who bond with and love the animals, and for whom the animals may represent a sole focus or major focus for their lives. Our next argument is based on the fact that the major target for the most onerous breed-specific legislation (such as Denver's) are "pit bulls" and pit bulls are not even identifiable as a breed!

Historically, the term "pit bull" has identified three breeds; the American Staffordshire Terrier, the American Pit Bull Terrier, and the Staffordshire Bull Terrier. If one goes to Google and types in "Find the Pit Bull," one can find more than 25 breeds that have been called "pit bulls."

It appears that a pit bull is a dog that meets someone's a priori notion of a pit bull. There is no genetic test for "pit-bullness." Thus breed-specific laws targeting pit bulls are reminiscent of a Colorado city ordinance allowing police to shoot a vicious dog on sight, where a vicious dog was defined as "One who is vicious." The infamous Denver law in fact defines a pit bull as one of the three breeds mentioned earlier, or "any dog displaying the majority of the physical traits of one or more of those breeds."

All of this leaves aside the obvious question of "pit bull crosses." Given that all the purebreds identified above can be viewed as "pit bulls," what of pit bull mixes? Once again it would seem that it is a pit bull if someone views it as a pit bull. Given that there is no genetic trait of pit bullness and, even if there were, there is no objective, scientific way to determine what proportion of such "mixed blood," is definitive for being designated a pit bull under restrictive legislation, we find ourselves using pit bull as an emotive/evaluative term that tells us more about our fears than about any objective traits in the animals.

Historically, it stands to reason that pit bulls, as fighting dogs, were culled if they were aggressive to humans, since handlers needed to separate them. That argument in itself says little, as breeds can change in relatively short time. This is manifest when great popularity of a breed eventuates in its deterioration as dogs are bred indiscriminately—this has happened to collies when "Lassie" came out, German shepherds, Saint Bernards, and others.

An objective measure of temperament is the breed testing done by the American Temperament Testing Society, a nonprofit group that evaluates the temperament of dogs by a uniform test. In the 2006 tests, 84.1 percent of American Pit Bull Terriers passed the test, 83.9 percent of American Staffordshires, and 85.2 percent of Staffordshire Terriers. In contrast, only 71.4 percent of Chihuahuas passed, 79.2 percent of Collies, and 75.5 percent of Pomeranians passed. This, of course, must be taken with a grain of salt, as the numbers tested of each breed varied widely. But it helps belie the view that all pit bulls are vicious.

In fact, any dog can be made vicious by owners, depending on treatment. Beating the animal, tying it on a short leash, failing to socialize, and many other ways of managing the animal can make a dog mean or a biter. Breed reputations are garnered largely by public hysteria fueled by the media. At various points German shepherds, Dobermans, and Saint Bernards were "killer dog of the year." In fact, I adopted a wonderful Doberman whose owner relinquished her because she was getting older and "everyone knows their brains get too big for their skulls and they get mean."

All of this gets us to a major point: there is nothing wrong with laws restricting vicious dogs, but the individual dog should have demonstrated uncontrolled aggressive behavior before it is seized. And the system should punish the owner severely, not merely destroy the dog, for it is owners that typically train for aggression, or fail to control it. In fact, recent data indicates that owners who have animals identified as "pit bulls" have more criminal histories than do owners of any other sort of dog. Such ordinances are not morally or logically sound if they target arbitrarily designated groups rather than problematic individuals.

On a personal note: I have had a Rottweiler, two Dobermans, a pit bull cross, and an attack-trained German shepherd tied up most of his life in a junkyard. He let a turkey sleep on his head. Children rode the pit bull cross. The Dobermans were wonderful with children. The Rottweiler—weighing 160 pounds—approaches all strangers with his ball. The only truly mean dog who hated strangers was my Chihuahua cross, who would have been a true menace had she weighed more than six pounds. Given her size, she was a menace only to grasshoppers. Ironically, every one of these dogs except the Chihuahua could have been seized or destroyed under some breed-specific law. This in turn would suggest that dog size is a morally relevant consideration for destroying an innocent animal. That is morally intolerable on all the levels we have described.

Chapter 1

Introduction

JOAN E. SCHAFFNER

There are close to 74 million dogs living in the United States. A recent poll revealed that approximately 70 percent of Americans view their pets as members of their families. These animals are lucky. Their owners love and care for them, have them spayed or neutered, never chain them up but take them for walks on leashes, and avoid circumstances that might frighten or anger them while in the presence of other animals or strangers.

Other dogs, those with irresponsible owners, are not so lucky. They may be kept as "guard" dogs, left out in the weather with little shelter, tied up in the yard for days on end, or, worse still, used to fight. Others are allowed to roam freely, getting into dangerous situations that might trigger their instinct to attack. These are the dogs and owners that incite media attention and public hysteria, with legislators often reacting by passing "dangerous dog" ordinances.

The reality is that fatal dog attacks are very rare. In 2006, for example, there were 31 fatal dog attacks in the United States. In comparison, on average each year, 100 people are killed by lightning, 150 by falling coconuts, 54 by bug bites, and 65 by being struck by a cow. The root causes of fatal dog attacks have been fairly well established: Unsterilized dogs were involved in 97 percent of fatal attacks; reckless owners who abused, neglected, chained, and/or failed to properly supervise their dog in 84 percent; and guard dogs, yard dogs, or fighting dogs in 78 percent of these incidents. Dog attacks are injurious to the public health and safety, and they should be addressed by reasonable, fair, and effective legislation; however, many laws do not target these root causes and thus fail to adequately address the problem of dangerous dogs and their reckless owners. Moreover, some laws have been ruled unconstitutional because they infringe on the rights of owners.

These laws in turn create difficulties for enforcement. When a dog injures another human or animal, the authorities have the power to declare the dog "dangerous or vicious," seize it, and ultimately kill it under certain circumstances. Often the owner is not penalized at all (other than having the dog seized and killed). Several important issues arise, including the factors that trigger a finding of dangerousness, the gathering of proper evidence to prove the identity of the dog and the circumstances surrounding the incident, proper notice to the owner and an opportunity for the owner to defend the finding of "dangerous," and the handling of the dog during the proceedings.

These incidents and how the law addresses them also raise problems in the private sector for dog owners. In particular, it is not uncommon for dog owners to have to choose between their dog and their home; they may be unable to obtain homeowners insurance because of the breed of their dog, or prohibited from owning certain breeds of dog (or perhaps any dog) pursuant to the private covenants that govern their homeowners' association.

This book is designed to discuss the handling of dangerous dogs by the law and private associations. The authors explain why breed discrimination is immoral, unfair, and ineffective; discuss progressive approaches to better handle reckless owners and their dogs; and share strategies for prosecuting and defending dangerous dog cases.

In philosopher Bernard Rollin's foreword, he describes the moral theory underlying the treatment of animals as individual beings with independent interests and demonstrates how breed-discriminatory laws are conceptually flawed. Ledy VanKavage, an expert on dangerous dog legislation with Best Friends Animal Sanctuary, and Professor Joan Schaffner of the George Washington University Law School discuss dangerous dog legislation and several emerging issues involving these laws, including whether breed-discriminatory laws are fair and effective, the effect of recent advances that now help determine the breed of dogs based on their DNA, and the proven effective approaches to muzzling dangerous dogs and regulating their reckless owners. Professor

Joan Schaffner closes this section with an analysis of the constitutional challenges to breed-discriminatory laws including those raising vagueness, procedural due process, and substantive due process claims. In Part II, Enforcing and Defending Dangerous Dog Laws, Virginia prosecutor Michelle Welch and Florida defense attorney Marcy La Hart, both of whom have extensive expertise in dangerous dog cases, share their trial strategies. Part III focuses on the discrimination in the private homeownership sector: David Furlow, a senior partner at Thompson & Knight, presents effective strategies for challenging restrictive covenants and Professor Larry Cunningham of St. John's University School of Law explores, from scientific, legal, and policy standpoints, the practice of breed discrimination by insurance companies.

We hope this book will help advance the discussion on how best to protect all animals—human and nonhuman alike—in a fair, effective, and ethical manner.

Part I

Dangerous Dog Laws

Chapter 2

Ordinances Targeting Reckless Owners and Damaged Dogs: Is Canine Profiling Effective?

LEDY VANKAVAGE AND JOAN E. SCHAFFNER

Mark Twain said, "What gets us into trouble is not what we don't know, it's what we know for sure that just ain't so."

If you read the paper lately, every dog that bit must be a "pit." Because of a plethora of media attention singling out American pit bull terriers as the new dangerous dog du jour, some city councils have passed laws banning any mixed-breed dog that merely resembles an American pit bull terrier.[1] Some cities are even expanding the number of breeds and mixes banned from their jurisdictions.[2]

These key questions need to be addressed:

> Are breed-discriminatory laws a rational public-safety response to dog bites?

> What definitive tests exist to determine a dog's heritage?

> Now that scientific advances have made DNA testing available to determine the heritage of mixed-breed dogs, should cities that have breed-discriminatory ordinances be required to conduct DNA tests on dogs without papers to prove their bloodlines?

---

1. *See, e.g.*, Prince George's County Code § 3-185.01 (banning pit bulls).

2. *See, e.g.*, Dog Laws at Large, Breeds, Mixes, "look-a-Likes", All Banned (Aug. 8, 2007), http://doglawsatlarge.blogspot.com/2007/08/breeds-mixes-look-likes-all-banned.html (listing several cities that have banned or are considering banning multiple breeds of dogs, including pits, Rottweilers, Dobermans, chows, Akitas, and cane corsos).

> What are effective approaches to addressing reckless owners and dangerous dogs?

> Is there liability for veterinarians, police officers, or animal-control wardens who wrongly identify a dog as a member of a breed without DNA testing and deprive an owner of his or her property (i.e., pet) without due process?

Welcome to the emerging field of reckless owner and dangerous dog laws.

What Is a Pit Bull?

Simply put, there is no such breed. There are American Pit Bull Terriers, American bulldogs, American Staffordshire Terriers, bull terriers, bull-dogs, bullmastiffs, Boston terriers, boxers, French bulldogs, and Stafford-shire Bull Terriers. In some communities with breed-discriminatory laws, any muscular short-haired dog is deemed a "pit bull" if a dog warden or cop says it is.

Werewolf, Lassie, or Just Plain Dog?

For thousands of years, dogs have helped man, and man has helped dogs—a working symbiotic relationship. The heroics and loyalty of *Canis lupus familiaris* have earned the dog the enviable title of man's best friend.

Given that lengthy and strong relationship between humans and dogs, is it rational for cities to fear and discriminate against a dog based on its breed and not its temperament?

According to Janis Bradley, author of "Dogs Bite, but Balloons and Slippers Are More Dangerous," more people are killed by lightning each year than by dogs. According to the American Pet Products Association, the dog population has blossomed to more than 74.8 million canines in the United States.[3] Despite the increase in the number of dogs in the United States, deaths from dog attacks are exceedingly rare and have not increased over the last two decades—25 fatalities were reported in

---

3. Am. Pet Products Ass'n, 2007–2008 APPA National Pet Owners Survey, http://americanpetproducts.org/pubs_survey.asp.

1990 as compared to 24 in 2008. However, the number of fatalities fluctuates from year to year.[4]

Why the hysteria regarding dogs when swimming pools and SUVs are much more dangerous? The reality is that dogs, like cats, are carnivores, and humans' primal fear of predators often results in bad laws. Breed discrimination appears to have its origin from those who misrepresent a report published in the September 15, 2000 issue of the *Journal of the American Veterinary Medical Association*. The article was entitled "Breeds of Dogs Involved in Fatal Human Attacks in the United States Between 1979 and 1998."[5] In contrast to what has been reported in the news media, the data contained within the report cannot be used to infer any breed-specific risk for dog-bite fatalities.[6] Indeed, more than 25 breeds were involved in fatal human attacks over the 20-year period summarized in the report. Moreover, the authors themselves concluded the article by stating:

> Only with numerator and denominator data and with formal evaluations of the impacts of strategies tried by various communities will we be able to make science-based recommendations for decreasing the number of dog bites. In the interim, adequate funding for animal control agencies, enforcement of existing animal control laws, and educational and policy strategies to reduce inappropriate dog and owner behaviors will likely result in benefits to communities and may well decrease the number of dog bites that occur."[7]

Many breed-discriminatory laws are enacted allegedly to protect children. Are some dog breeds more frequent biters of children? A study reported in the *Journal of Injury Prevention* revealed that dogs that bite children have often not bitten children before, but they tend to have

---

4. *See* NCRC, Types of Dog Bites at http://nationalcanineresearchcouncil.com/dog-bites/types-of-dog-bites/.

5. J.J. Sacks et al, *Breeds of Dogs Involved in Fatal Human Attacks in the United States Between 1979 and 1998*, 217 J. AM. VET. MED. ASSOC. 836–40 (2000).

6. *See infra* Chapter 7 (discussing the problems with dog-bite statistics, Larry Cunningham concludes, "It is for these reasons that CDC scientists and other researchers have concluded that dog-bite statistics are incomplete and should not be used by legislatures, insurance companies, or other decision-makers to make categorical judgments about particular breeds of dog.). *See also* Toledo v. Tellings, 2006 WL 513946, at *4 (Ohio App. 6 Dist.), *rev'd*, 871 N.E.2d 1152 (Ohio 2007) (reliance on bare statistics without referencing total number of dogs in each dog breed has "no relevance or meaning").

7. Sacks et al., *supra* note 5, at 840.

underlying behavioral or medical problems.[8] The research team analyzed the circumstances surrounding 111 cases of dog bites involving 103 dogs over a period of four years. All 103 dogs involved had bitten children and had been referred to the same veterinary behavior clinic. The findings indicated that food guarding was the most common circumstance involving children familiar to the dog; territory guarding was the most common involving children unknown to the dog. Interestingly, most of the dogs had been neutered and more than half had taken obedience-training classes. While the analysis highlighted distinctive patterns of behavior, no particular breed was distinctive in its characteristics.

But do not most American pit bull terriers have bad temperaments? Actually, no. The American Temperament Test Society (ATTS) has developed a test to measure certain psychological attributes in dogs.

The ATTS describes its test as follows:

> The ATTS Temperament Test focuses on and measures different aspects of temperament such as stability, shyness, aggressiveness, and friendliness as well as the dog's instinct for protectiveness towards its handler and/or self-preservation in the face of a threat.
>
> The test simulates a casual walk through a park or neighborhood where everyday life situations are encountered. During this walk, the dog experiences visual, auditory and tactile stimuli. Neutral, friendly and threatening situations are encountered, calling into play the dog's ability to distinguish between non-threatening situations and those calling for watchful and protective reactions.
>
> Dogs must be at least 18 months old to enter this test. The test takes about eight to 12 minutes to complete. The dog is on a loose six-foot (6′) lead. The handler is not allowed to talk to the dog, give commands, or give corrections.
>
> Failure on any part of the test is recognized when a dog shows:
>
> ❯ Unprovoked aggression
> ❯ Panic without recovery
> ❯ Strong avoidance[9]

---

8. Ilana Reisner, Francis Schofer & Michael Nance, *Behavioral Assessment of Child-Directed Canine Aggression*, 13 INJURY PREVENTION 348–51 (2007).

9. Am. Temperament Test Soc'y, Description of the Temperament Test, http://www .atts.org/testdesc.html.

The ATTS breed statistics show that breeds of dogs typically falling into the illusive category of "pit bull," such as American Pit Bull Terrier and American Staffordshire Terrier, consistently scored above average for all breeds tested, year in and year out.[10]

A quick scroll through any online governmental dangerous dog registry shows that dangerous dogs come in all shapes, sizes, and breeds.[11] So why do legislators target pit bulls?

Karen Delise, a veterinary technician, author of *The Pitbull Placebo* and *Fatal Dog Attacks*, and founder and director of research for the National Canine Research Council, examined media bias in dog-bite reporting. She surveyed news stories regarding dog attacks that occurred during four days in August 2007. The result is disconcerting.

> August 18: A Labrador mix attacked a 70-year-old man, sending him to the hospital in critical condition. Police officers arrived at the scene, and the dog was shot after charging the officers. This incident was reported in one article in the local paper.

> August 19: A 16-month-old child received fatal head and neck injuries after being attacked by a mixed-breed dog. This attack was reported in two articles in the local paper.

> August 20: A six-year-old boy was hospitalized after having his ear torn off and receiving severe bites to the head by a medium-size mixed-breed dog. This attack was reported in one article in the local paper.

> August 21: A 59-year-old woman was attacked in her home while trying to break up a dogfight involving her neighbor's Jack Russell terrier and two pit bulls. The pit bulls had broken off their chains and followed her neighbor's Jack Russell terrier in through her doggy door. She was hospitalized with severe injuries. Her dog was not injured. This attack was reported in more than 230 articles in national and international newspapers, and on major television news networks, including CNN, MSNBC, and Fox.[12]

10. Am. Temperament Test Soc'y, Breed Statistics, http://www.atts.org/statistics.html.
11. *See, e.g.,* Va. Dep't Agric. & Consumer Servs., Virginia Dangerous Dog Registry, http://www.virginia.gov/vdacs_dd/public/cgi-bin/public.cgi.
12. Nat'l Canine Research Council (NCRC), The Pit Bull Paparazzi (2007), http://nationalcanineresearchcouncil.com/wp-content/uploads/2009/01/paparazzincrc.pdf.

Thus, during those four days in August 2007, four dog attacks made the news—including a fatality involving a mixed-breed dog—but only the incident involving the pit bulls garnered intense national media attention.

Given the pervasive media bias,[13] as illustrated by the above example, it isn't a surprise that city councils ask their attorneys to research and draft ordinances to protect the public from certain breeds of dogs. However, the challenge to attorneys is to research what proactive ordinances are effective in protecting the public and to allow sufficient due process for the owners of the dogs. Dogs, after all, are property—actually, they're property-plus because of our strong emotional attachment to our pets—and ordinances should not infringe on property rights.

The "CSI" Effect: Doggy DNA and Its Impact on Breed-Discriminatory Laws

Attorneys know that proof matters. Thanks to the television program *CSI*, juries and judges love, and now often expect, DNA evidence in paternity and criminal cases. Doggy DNA is now starting to affect individual breed determinations and could shape the drafting of animal ordinances.

In the fall of 2007, DNA blood testing became available through laboratories such as BioPet Vet Lab, a division of EDP Biotech,[14] and MMI Genomics,[15] developer of the Canine Heritage Breed test to determine a dog's lineage. This scientific advance is already being used in individual breed identification cases and could eventually play a role in overturning breed-discriminatory ordinances. In Kansas City, Kansas, for example, a man won his eight-month legal battle with the city to keep his dog, Niko, after DNA testing proved Niko wasn't a "pit bull," as the animal control wardens had stated. Niko was housed at animal control for the entire eight months of the court case, at a great cost to

---

13. *See, e.g.,* NCRC, Audience Interest, http://nationalcanineresearchcouncil.com/dog-bites/dog-bites-and-the-media/audience-interest/.
14. BioPet Vet Lab, http://biopetvetlab.com/index.htm.
15. Metamorphix, Inc., http://www.metamorphixinc.com/about6.html.

Niko, his owners, and the town taxpayers. Niko, a mixed-breed dog, is now back home after the ordeal.[16] Many breed-discriminatory laws were passed before the advent of DNA testing for dog breeds. Unfortunately many attorneys are unaware that DNA testing for breeds even exists. This scientific advance could make breed-discriminatory ordinances susceptible to a legal challenge if the dog in question is not registered with the American Kennel Club (AKC) or the United Kennel Club (UKC) as a certain breed. Attorneys drafting a breed-discriminatory law at the behest of their city council should take DNA evidence into account and determine how the city might pay for the testing to prove that a mixed-breed or unregistered dog is of a certain lineage. This gives a whole new meaning to the phrase "Let me see your papers."

The State of Iowa's Citizens' Aide/Ombudsman revealed problems with the identification of breeds in a November 15, 2006, report concerning Maquoketa's pit bull ban ordinance and enforcement.[17] Kelli Wilsef owned a mixed-breed dog that a police officer identified as a pit bull; the city council, relying on the testimony of two law enforcement officers but no veterinarian or other expert on dog breeds, concluded that Wilsef's dog was a pit bull mix. The ombudsman concluded that the city council did not have sufficient evidence of the dog's breed. This 2006 opinion was handed down prior to the advent of DNA testing to determine a dog's heritage. Today, an enlightened city council would likely refer to the available DNA tests.

Liability Questions

Now that DNA testing is available to more accurately determine a dog's breed, owners of dogs determined to be a "pit bull" without verification through DNA testing may have claims for relief if their dog is harmed

---

16. Tess Koppelman, Fox 4 News (WDAF-TV), *Man Wins Dog Back After DNA Test Proves Dog Isn't Pit Bull*, Fox4kc.com (Feb. 13, 2008), http://www.fox4kc.com/wdaf-manwinsdogbackafterdnate-5757542,0,6242076.story.

17. Investigation of Maquoketa's Pit Bull Ban Ordinance and Enforcement by the State of Iowa Citizens' Aide/Ombudsman, Case File 0603634 (Nov. 15, 2006).

as a result of an inaccurate identification.[18] For example, what if a purported "pit bull" is seized and killed by the city for failure to comply with the law banning pit bulls, but the city fails to do DNA testing or even employ a veterinarian or AKC or UKC judge to determine the dog's breed? Indeed, what training or certification do law enforcement officers or animal control wardens or, in some cases, the experts they rely upon, have to prove that they are experts in breed identification?

Section 1983 of the U.S. Code provides a remedy for individuals whose federal constitutional or statutory rights are violated by state actors.[19] Dog owners have challenged breed-discriminatory laws, sometimes successfully, arguing that the law is overly vague for failure to adequately define the term "pit bull." Such vagueness violates their rights to due process by providing insufficient notice to owners and insufficient guidance to local authority to accurately and fairly classify dogs under the definition. This in turn leads to arbitrary and discriminatory enforcement.[20]

With DNA testing available to more accurately classify the breed of dog, these owners may have another argument for arbitrary and discriminatory enforcement of the law if the local authority fails to verify the dog's breed through a DNA test. Although the official may have a defense of qualified immunity[21] initially, once DNA testing becomes commonplace, identifying the dog's breed based solely on appearance will no longer suffice as reasonable, especially if the result is harm or death to the dog. Moreover, if the jurisdiction fails to adequately train its officers on the use of DNA testing, the municipality may be held

---

18. A complete and thorough analysis of potential claims is beyond the scope of this text.

19. 42 U.S.C. § 1983 states, "Every person who, under color of any statute, ordinance, regulation, custom, or usage, of any State or Territory or the District of Columbia, subjects, or causes to be subjected, any citizen of the United States or other person within the jurisdiction thereof to the deprivation of any rights, privileges, or immunities secured by the Constitution and laws, shall be liable to the party injured in an action at law, suit in equity, or other proper proceeding for redress." This statute allows private suits for damages against officials and municipalities without violating the 11th Amendment because the suit is not against the state, per se, but against an individual.

20. *See infra* Chapter 3 (analysis of constitutional challenges to breed-discriminatory laws).

21. An official may argue qualified immunity if his or her conduct does not violate clearly established rights of which a reasonable person would have known. *Harlow v. Fitzgerald*, 457 U.S. 800, 818 (1982).

liable as well. In fact, private veterinarians who determine the breed of a dog based solely on appearance may be subject to suit for malpractice if their identification is then used by local authorities to harm the dog. The outcome for the jurisdiction will be increased cost to verify the dog's breed in order to properly enforce the law and/or increased cost of litigation defending suits for failure to do so. Given that breed-discriminatory laws have already proven both ineffective and inefficient, this new wrinkle is yet another argument for enacting nondiscriminatory laws to regulate owners and their dogs.

What Do the Studies Show: Are Canine-Profiling Laws Effective?

It is difficult to assess the effectiveness or ineffectiveness of breed-discriminatory legislation due to a dearth of studies on the topic. Ideally such studies would be conducted over long periods of time both before and after legislation is implemented. To date, there are no studies showing that breed-discriminatory laws protect the public. There are only two published studies on the topic and none in the United States.

The first study involves the United Kingdom's Dangerous Dog Act, which banned "pit bulls" in 1991.[22] The Klaassen study concluded that the ban had no effect on stopping dog attacks. However, it is important to note that a relatively brief period of time (one three-month period just prior to the enactment of the law and another three-month period two year after its enactment) was assessed in this study. The study also involved only incidents seen at one urban accident and emergency department before the implementation of the Act and again two years later.

The second, more recent, study compared dog bites reported to the public health department of Aragon, Spain, for the five-year period before the introduction of the city's Dangerous Dog Act in 1999 and the five-year period after its introduction.[23] The study deals only with

---

22. B. Klaassen, J.R. Buckley & A. Esmail, *Does the Dangerous Dogs Act Protect Against Animal Attacks: A Prospective Study of Mammalian Bites in the Accident and Emergency Department*, 27(2) INJURY 89–91 (1996).

23. B. Rosado et al., *Spanish Dangerous Animals Act: Effect of the Epidemiology of Dog Bites*, 2(5) J. VET. BEHAVIOR 166–74 (2007).

medically attended dog bites. The 2001 census showed Aragon with a population of 1,204,215 inhabitants. The registered population of dogs total 15,593, of which 4.2 percent belonged to the allegedly dangerous breeds, including Rottweiler, Argentine dogo, Brazilian mastiff, Tosa Inu, Akita Inu, pit bull terrier, Staffordshire bull terrier, and American Staffordshire terrier. These allegedly dangerous breeds accounted for 2.4 percent of the dog bites before the breed-discriminatory law was introduced and 3.5 percent of the dog bites after the breed-discriminatory law was introduced. These statistics show that these breeds accounted for very few bites before and after the law but interestingly their percentage increased slightly after the breed-discriminatory law was enacted. The authors state that the "results suggest that BSL was fundamentally flawed . . . [and] not effective in protecting people from dog bites in a significant manner."[24]

As with the Klaassen study, the Aragon results suggest that the introduction of the Dangerous Dog Act was unsuccessful in the attempt to reduce the number of people injured by dog bites. Not surprisingly, the most popular breeds of dogs were the main biting breeds.

These conclusions are further reinforced by a recent newspaper article discussing the effect of the Denver, Colorado, pit bull ban enacted in 1989 after the tragic mauling of a Denver resident by a pit bull.[25] Twenty years later, the Denver Animal Control Director admits that he is unable to say with any certainty whether the ban itself has made Denver any safer. What the city does know is that Labrador retrievers are the most likely dog to bite (they are also the most popular dog in the city) and that Denver is less safe than Boulder, a city with dangerous dog laws that do not target a specific breed but focus on the education and regulation of dog owners.[26] Between 1995 and 2006, Denver had almost six times as many dog-related hospitalizations as Boulder, even though Denver's population is less than twice that of Boulder.[27]

---

24. *Id.* at 172.
25. Peter Marcus, *Do Dog Breed Bans Work?*, DENVER DAILY NEWS, Mar. 3, 2009, *available at* http://www.thedenverdailynews.com/article.php?aID=3473.
26. *Id.* (referring to data provided by the Colorado Association of Animal Control Officers and released by the Coalition for Living Safely with Dogs).
27. *Id.*

The Denver Health Department plans to consider changing the law in light of this data.

According to Karen Delise, the fatal dog attacks that occurred in the United States in 2006 had these commonalities:

> 97 percent of the owners did not neuter or spay their dogs.

> 84 percent of the attacks involved owners who abused or neglected their dogs, failed to contain their dogs or chained their dogs, or left their dogs unsupervised when they were allowed to interact with children.

> 78 percent of the owners did not maintain their dogs as pets (they were used as guard, breeding, yard, or fighting dogs).[28]

According to Delise, there is no documented case of a single, neutered, house pet American pit bull terrier causing a human fatality. These observations strongly suggest that instead of drafting breed-discriminatory laws, attorneys would serve their city council better by targeting the owners who allow these commonalities to occur—reckless owners who abuse, neglect, chain, improperly supervise, or fail to neuter their dog, as well as those who keep their dogs for purposes other than companionship. As Delise says, "Dogs are the property, for better or for worse, of their owners. . . . You can't write a law that a dog is going to be able to read. You need to write laws that hold owners responsible for the behavior of their dogs and for them to have care and control of their dogs."[29] In fact, law enforcement has recognized for years that many fatal dog attacks are caused by the negligent, reckless, and even criminal behavior of the owners. In April 2009, a New York resident became the thirty-fourth dog owner in this country since 1980 to be convicted of manslaughter in a fatal dog attack case.[30]

A very recent study of the causes of dog aggression supports Delises' conclusions. A research team, lead by Joaquín Pérez-Guisado, from

---

28. NCRC, Types of Dog Bites, *at* http://nationalcanineresearchcouncil.com/dog-bites/types-of-dog-bites/.

29. Marcus, *supra* note 25 (quoting Karen Delise).

30. NCRC, Dog News, *New York Woman Becomes 34th Owner Convicted in a Case of a Fatal Dog Attack in the United States, at* http://nationalcanineresearchcouncil.com/dog-news/

the University of Córdoba (UCO) studied 711 dogs (354 males and 357 females) older than one year of age of which 594 were purebred and 117 were half-breed dogs.[31] A wide range of breeds were observed, including the American Pit Bull Terrier, the Labrador Retriever, the Chihuahua, and the Irish Setter. The study, published in the *Journal of Animal and Veterinary Advances* in 2009, concluded that the breed of dog "has little to do with a dog's aggressive behavior compared to all the owner-dependant factors"[32] associated with the dog's care, handling, and training. Specifically, the researchers determined that while "certain breeds, male sex, a small size, or an age of between 5–7 years old, are 'the dog-dependent factors associated with greater dominance aggression,' . . . these factors have 'minimal effect' on whether the dog behaves aggressively. Factors linked to the owner's actions are more influential."[33]

Cities and states taking a community approach to find creative, practical solutions to decrease the number of bites in their community are beginning to focus on the crux of the problem, these reckless owners.

The Other End of the Leash: A New Breed of Law Targeting Reckless Owners

Given the ineffectiveness of laws that target breeds and the recognition that the owner generally is the culpable party whose conduct can be affected by the law, jurisdictions are finding it more fair and effective to target the reckless owners, not the dogs.

Restricting Dog Ownership by Certain High-Risk Persons

It makes sense to restrict or even ban high-risk owners from owning a dog. Just as gun ownership is a constitutional right in our country but nevertheless can be restricted in appropriate circumstances, as in

---

31. Science Daily, Science News, *Dogs Are Aggressive If They Are Trained Badly*, May 1, 2009 (citing Joaquín Pérez-Guisado & Andres Muñoz-Serrano, *Factors Linked to Dominance Aggression in Dogs*, 8 (2) JOURNAL OF ANIMAL AND VETERINARY ADVANCES, 336–342 (2009)) *at* http://www.sciencedaily.com/releases/2009/04/090424114315.htm.

32. *Id.*

33. *Id.* A model has been developed to provide estimates of the fiscal impact of breed-discriminatory legislation on communities. It is available at www.bestfriends.org/BDLfiscalimpact.

the case of convicted felons, the same can be true for dog ownership, especially if the dogs might be used as a weapon.

In 2006, Illinois became the first state to restrict felons from owning unsterilized dogs.[34] As noted above, unsterilized dogs have been found to be involved in the majority of bites. So, in the Land of Lincoln, convicted felons can own whatever breed of dog they want as long as it is sterilized and microchipped for permanent identification.

The law makes it a misdemeanor for those convicted of forcible felonies, felony gun charges, drug charges, or felony violations of the Humane Care for Animals Act to own any unsterilized dog or dog that has been declared "vicious" by a court under the Illinois Animal Control Act.[35] The year the law took effect, the ASPCA helped the Illinois Department of Corrections train all of their parole agents in the new law. Host families are informed of the need to sterilize their dog before a felon can reside with them after their release from prison.

In 2007, the city of St. Paul, Minnesota, passed an ordinance targeting reckless dog owners.[36] St. Paul pet owners cited more than once for abusing or neglecting an animal are legally prohibited from owning another pet under the ordinance. The law targets pet owners who train their dogs to fight, puppy-mill operators, and reckless dog owners. Reckless dog owners cannot register a new animal if their dogs are removed twice in a five-year span. City law requires all dogs more than three months old to have a license that costs $50 a year; the cost is reduced to $10 a year if the animal is spayed or neutered.

Also in 2007, the city of Tacoma, Washington, created an ordinance regulating "Problem Pet Owners."[37] A person who commits three or more animal-control violations in a 24-month period could be declared a problem pet owner and forced to surrender all of his or her animals.

---

34. 720 ILL. COMP. STAT. 5/12-36.
35. 510 ILL. COMP. STAT. 5 *et seq.*
36. ST. PAUL MUN. CODE § 200.02: License Required, *available at* http://www.municode.com/Resources/gateway.asp?pid=10061&sid=23.
37. City of Tacoma news (Dec. 9, 2007), *available at* http://www.cityoftacoma.org/Page.aspx?hid=7650 (members of the City Council to hear final reading of the ordinance that would set penalties and define owners who repeatedly violate animal control laws as "problem pet owners").

In 2008 numerous bills outlawing a variety of dog breeds were introduced and defeated. Through the legislative process one strong public safety measure focusing on reckless owners emerged. On May 15, 2008, the governor of Minnesota signed into law a bill that prohibits convicted owners from residing with dogs in the state again.[38] This generic dangerous dog bill takes the focus off of the dog and places it squarely on the owner. Dog ownership is prohibited if a person has been convicted of a third or subsequent violation of the registration, maintenance, or microchipping provisions of the dangerous dog law.[39] A Minnesotan who has been convicted of manslaughter involving an animal or harm caused by a dog is also forbidden from owning a dog.[40] Moreover, the law applies to owners whose dog was ordered destroyed under the dangerous dog law and been convicted of one or more sections of the law. Members residing in the household are also prohibited from owning a dog. Review of the prohibition is allowed in certain cases.

Taking a Community-Policing Approach to Reckless Owners and Dangerous Dogs

Calgary, Alberta, does not discriminate against particular breeds of dogs but focuses on protecting the public from all aggressive dogs regardless of breed. The city's bylaw enforcement animal control officers adopt a community-policing/problem-solving approach when dealing with members of the public. The focus is on stiff fines and public education. The city encourages its wardens to get out of their trucks and talk with folks. If a dog bites a person, a $350 fine is imposed; if the person bitten needs medical attention, the fine increases to $750. There is also a $250 fine for a dog-on-dog attack or an unlicensed pooch.[41] Since Calgary enacted and enforced this new aggressive-dog ordinance, the city has experienced a 56 percent decline in aggressive-dog incidents and a 21 percent decline in biting incidents in just two years.[42]

---

38. Minn. H.F. 2906, 85th Sess. (Feb. 14, 2008), amending MINN. STAT. §§ 347.50–.56.
39. MINN. STAT. §§ 347.51, 347.515, 347.52.
40. Id. §§ 609.205 (4), 609.226 1, 609.226 2.
41. City of Calgary, Responsible Pet Ownership Bylaw (Bylaw 23M2006 as amended by 48M2008, 49M2008).
42. Amanda Gleason, Letter to the Editor, *Campaign Against Pit Bulls in Whitehall Is Sorely Lacking in Facts*, COLUMBUS DISPATCH, June 21, 2008, *available at* http://www.dispatch

Most recently, Italy decided to "scrap its blacklist of dangerous dogs."[43] Beginning in April 2009, no longer will seventeen breeds of dog be deemed dangerous per se in that country. Instead, the new law focuses on education, requiring a short training course for prospective dog owners, and places the onus on the owners to properly train and control their dog.

Restricting Tethering and Chaining

According to Delise, 25 percent of all fatal attacks since the 1960s have been inflicted by chained dogs.[44] Chaining may make a dog fearful, unsocialized, or territorial. In essence, tethering "invites" situations where aggression may be the only response a dog has. Instead of banning a breed, for instance, Lawrence, Kansas, restricts chaining unattended pets outside.[45] In Lawrence, a person can tether a dog for no longer than one hour. Since the city has enacted the ordinance, abuse, neglect, and dog-fighting complaints have dropped significantly.[46] Some states, including Texas, have adopted chaining restrictions. Texas prohibits dogs being tied up, chained, or tethered under any of the following conditions:

> Between the hours of 10 p.m. and 6 a.m.
> Within 500 feet of school property.
> When the temperature is below 32 degrees.
> When a heat advisory or ozone alert has been issued.
> When a pinch, choke, or improperly fitting nylon collar is used.[47]

Restricting chaining between the hours of 10 p.m. and 6 a.m. can also reduce the number of barking complaints.

.com/live/content/editorials/stories/2008/06/21/Gleason__SAT_ART_06-21-08_A11_K9AHOP5.html?sid=101.

43. *Italy Scraps Dangerous Dog Blacklist* (Mar 3, 2009) *at* http://www.lifeinitaly.com/node/4229.

44. Karen Delise, Fatal Dog Attacks: The Stories Behind the Statistics, 20, 23–25 (2002); Karen Delise, The Pit Bull Placebo: The Media, Myths and Politics of Canine Aggression, 162 (2007).

45. Code City of Lawrence Kan. § 3-105 (picketing of dogs).

46. Mike Belt, *Dog Fighting, Animal Cruelty Cases on Decline*, LJWorld.com, Sept. 6, 2006, *available at* http://www2.ljworld.com/news/2006/sep/06dog_fighting_animal_cruelty_cases_decline/.

47. Tex. Health and Safety Code ch. 821.

Pack Mentality

Some states, cities, and counties have pet-population-control programs to combat the real problem of packs of dogs. In Illinois, the Anna Cieslewicz Act,[48] named for a woman who was killed by two intact abandoned male dogs living in the Dan Ryan Woods in Chicago, created a pet-population-control fund to allow poor people to have their dogs sterilized and vaccinated. The law also imposed public-safety fines on dog owners whose dog was found running at large or declared dangerous or vicious under the Illinois Animal Control Act. The public-safety fines go into the state pet-population-control fund.

The Illinois Animal Control Act also addresses packs of dogs. The law defines a "potentially dangerous dog" as a dog that is unsupervised and found running at large with three or more other dogs.[49] Potentially dangerous dogs have to be sterilized and microchipped for permanent identification. The "potentially dangerous" designation expires automatically after 12 months of the most recent violation of the section.

Requiring DNA of Deemed Dangerous Dogs

In addition to the spaying or neutering and microchipping of Level II Dangerous Dogs, Knox County, Tennessee, has gone high-tech. The county's ordinance requires that a sample from the "dangerous dog" be preserved for possible DNA testing and delivered to the animal-control division in case the animal is suspected of another bite.[50]

An Australian company, Genetic Technologies, has even created a dog-attack DNA kit to help preserve DNA evidence at the scene of a dog attack. Such DNA evidence may help investigators in several circumstances: when a dog-attack victim is unable to identify the exact dog; when a pack of dogs is involved and the specific biter needs to be identified; when a dog owner refuses to cooperate; or when domestic animals have been attacked with no witnesses to the event.

---

48. Ill. Pub. Act 94-0639.
49. 510 Ill. Comp. Stat. 5/2.17c.
50. Knox County Ordinance 0-07-12-102, at § 6–77 (mandatory restrictions on level two dangerous dogs) (2007).

Protecting the Public While Preserving Responsible Owners' Property Rights

Nondiscriminatory reckless owner and dangerous dog laws can protect the public and not infringe on the property rights of responsible owners. We can do better than to allow breed-discriminatory legislation to sever the human-animal bond and undermine the faith people have in their city government. According to a poll commissioned by Best Friends, 69 percent of Americans now view their pets as members of the family.[51]

The fear of pets being killed simply because of their breed has even permeated our schools. The 94th General Assembly of the State of Illinois passed House Resolution 1026[52]—the winner of a "best resolution" contest for schoolchildren. This winning resolution was submitted by students from Brentano Math and Science Academy in Chicago. H.R. 1026 states that dog control problems are created by people and are not limited to a breed or mix; singling out breeds of dogs as vicious or banning them only shifts the responsibility from the dog owner, where it belongs, to the breed of dog, and does not solve community dog problems. It was resolved that municipalities should be encouraged to address animal attacks by enforcing laws that encourage responsible and humane treatment of dogs and all other animals; teaching communities about responsible dog ownership, creating awareness, and punishing illegal dog fighting as effective strategies for keeping communities safe.

The anguish experienced by thousands of responsible owners who have their pets seized and killed simply because of their perceived breed was expressed movingly in an e-mail posted to several animal rescue groups on the web in 2006. The woman, a Florissant, Missouri resident, explained that she owned an 8-year-old neutered pit bull, Ali, and had just been made aware that pit bulls had been outlawed in her city and she had just missed the two-month grace period to register

---

51. Best Friends Animal Soc'y, Best Friends Kindness Index (June 23, 2006), http://network.bestfriends.org/campaigns/bfday/kindnessindex.aspx?.
52. H.R. 1026, 94th Gen. Assemb. of Ill., *available at* http://www.ilga.gov/legislation/BillStatus.asp?DocNum=1026&GAID=8&DocTypeID=HR&LegId=25446&SessionID=50&GA=94.

him as previously owned. City Hall would not grant any waivers, and if she did not move him out of the jurisdiction within one week, he would be confiscated and killed. She was devastated. She had bottle fed Ali since he was a pup and he had become her best friend. Ali was friendly to all—her new 8-month old baby, other dogs, and even cats. Ali had attended socialization classes and was a model canine citizen. Now he was to be taken from her just because he was a pit bull. How could the city be so coldhearted? She was willing to do anything to save him, including moving their family to another jurisdiction that did not discriminate against Ali. The message ended "He's been the one reliable, stable friend for so long, I don't know how I will manage without him. . . . I've lived in and supported this city almost my whole life, but I can't help but feel betrayed and bitter." Unfortunately we do not know what ever happened to Ali.[53]

Stories such as these demonstrate that we need a better solution to more effectively and fairly protect all citizens. School children should not have to worry about having their dogs taken from them and killed by their local government simply because of their appearance. Responsible dog owners should have the right to own whatever breed or mixed breed of dog they choose. The laws should fairly regulate the owners rather than discriminatorily target the breed.

To date, the statistics have failed to prove that breed-discriminatory laws are effective or efficient. In fact, such laws will become even more burdensome to enforce with the advent of DNA testing that will prevent officials from reasonably relying exclusively on "appearance" to identify a dog's breed. Jurisdictions with laws that target reckless owners and have safer neighborhoods have found their law "much more effective because it supplies them with additional tools to go after irresponsible owners, as well as educate the owners on their mistakes."[54]

---

53. Posting from Andrea Miller to animal rescue yahoo groups, "Owner has 7 days to 'get rid of' her wonderful dog! BSL Florissant, MO HELP!!!" (Mar. 11, 2006).

54. Marcus, *supra* note 25 (quoting Englewood Mayor Jim Woodward, who also said that his city decided against breed-specific legislation because the research he conducted indicated that banning pit bulls would not cut back on dog bites).

Chapter 3

The Constitutionality of Breed-Specific Legislation: A Summary

JOAN E. SCHAFFNER

To many, pit bulls are loving, loyal, family companions. To some, they are inherently dangerous beasts. In response, some politicians, catering to irrational fears of constituents, have enacted laws limiting or banning dogs based purely on their breed. As a practical matter these laws are ineffective and inefficient. As a legal matter they are unfair and possibly unconstitutional. Dog owners have brought constitutional challenges ranging from procedural due process to equal protection to constitutional takings. However, with the exception of a few enlightened courts, these challenges have failed.

This chapter summarizes the law in this area in the context of the 2007 case from Ohio addressing the constitutionality of breed-specific legislation (BSL), *Toledo v. Tellings.*[1] In 2006, the appellate court of Ohio found the Toledo BSL unconstitutional on a number of grounds. The decision was comprehensive, well-reasoned, and persuasive, and many advocates believed it might dictate the beginning of the end of such laws in the US. One year later, the Ohio Supreme Court, in a terse opinion, relying on decade-old precedent and unreliable statistics, reversed the appellate court.

---

1. 2006 WL 513946 (Ohio App. 6 Dist), *rev'd*, 871 N.E.2d 1152 (OH 2007).

Breed Discrimination:
Breed-Specific Legislation

There are four basic characteristics of breed-discriminatory laws relevant to a constitutional challenge: (1) definition of the breed; (2) procedures for identifying and challenging the designation; (3) ownership restrictions imposed; and (4) penalties for violation of the law.[2]

The legal definition of the breed is critical to an analysis of vagueness challenges. BSL defines the targeted breed in various ways from fairly specific to very general with many laws utilizing a combination of definitions. The most specific method to define the dogs is to name the breed, such as "American Pit Bull Terrier, American Staffordshire Terrier, and Staffordshire Terrier."[3] Beyond this, many statutes include one or more of the following additional categories: "any dog exhibiting those distinguishing characteristics which substantially conform to the standards established by the AKC or UKC for any of the stated breeds," "any dog displaying a majority of the physical traits of any one or more of the stated breeds," and/or "any dog which has the appearance and characteristics of any other breed commonly known as Pit Bull."[4] The more vague the definition, the greater the chance the court will find the statute void for vagueness.

The procedures for identifying the breed and for owners to challenge their dog's classification comprise a few basic factors relevant to a procedural due process challenge. Fundamental due process requires that a person be given adequate notice of the law and possible violation and a reasonable opportunity to be heard before being found in violation of the law. These requirements protect citizens from arbitrary and discriminatory enforcement. Most laws provide for animal control officers to determine whether the dog meets the definition of the breed using one or more of the definitions discussed. The guidelines provided to the officer for identifying the breed are relevant for finding the statute adequate to notify a person of the demands of the law. Adequate notice of a possible violation is determined based upon the nature and

---

2. Cynthia McNeely & Sarah Lindquist, *Dangerous Dog Laws: Failing to Give Man's Best Friend a Fair Shake at Justice*, 3 J. ANIMAL LAW 99, 112 (2007).

3. Colo. Dog Fanciers v. Denver, 820 P.2d 644, 646 (Co. 1991).

4. Am. Dog Owners Assoc. v. Des Moines, 469 N.W.2d 416, 418 (Iowa 1991).

timing of the notification and the opportunity to contest the classification. The specific provisions detailing these factors include: the service requirements for notifying the owner; whether a hearing to contest is provided and, if so, whether it is granted preseizure or postseizure of the dog; the party shouldering the burden of proof—the state or the owner; and the required burden of persuasion—preponderance of the evidence, clear and convincing evidence, or beyond a reasonable doubt.

BSL imposes various limitations on owners of dogs and may be relevant to takings challenges. The types of limitations range from heightened registration requirements, mandatory sterilization, muzzling of the dog when in public, special confinement parameters for housing the dog, and/or liability insurance, to a complete ban of the breed. When a ban is imposed, dogs owned at the time of enactment generally are grandfathered under the law but often must meet certain ownership limitations.

Finally, the nature of the penalty for violation is relevant to due process challenges since they determine whether the law is civil or criminal in nature. Citizens are due greater process before being criminally penalized. The penalties range from seizure and possible death of the dog to fines and possible imprisonment of the owner. Fines and imprisonment of the owner qualify as criminal penalties.

Tellings v. Toledo: A Rational Case Reversed

Tellings lived in Toledo and owned three pit bulls as family pets. The dogs had no history of aggression, violence, or other unlawful behavior.[5] One day while inspecting neighboring property, a health inspector saw the three pit bulls and reported Tellings to animal control. The inspector claimed Tellings was in violation of the local law that limited ownership to one "vicious" dog and mandated that the owner carry $100,000 liability insurance for such dog.[6] By statute, a "dog commonly known as a pit bull or pit bull mixed breed dog" was per se "vicious."[7]

---

5. Toledo v. Tellings, 2006 WL 513946, at *1 (Ohio App. 6 Dist.), *rev'd*, 871 N.E.2d 1152 (Ohio 2007).

6. *Id.*

7. Ohio Rev. Code § 955.11(A)(1)(a).

Since Tellings had three pit bulls, all deemed "vicious" under the law, and no liability insurance, he was found in violation of the law. He was allowed to keep one dog, he was able to find a home for the second dog, and the third was confiscated and killed by animal control.[8] Tellings filed suit challenging the constitutionality of the statute on numerous grounds.

Judicial Review

Judicial review of statutes is quite limited out of concern for separation of powers. It is well accepted that statutes are presumed constitutional with the burden upon the owner to prove unconstitutionality under a heightened standard of persuasion—either clear and convincing or beyond a reasonable doubt, depending upon the jurisdiction. Courts are not to substitute their judgment for the legislature but rather decide only if the law is rational when the law does not threaten fundamental rights or target a "suspect" class. Dogs are considered "qualified" property under the law[9] because of their "sometimes vicious and destructive qualities."[10] Statutes regulating dogs fall within the police power of the state to protect the health and safety of the public.[11] Thus, it is difficult to persuade a court that a statute regulating dog ownership is unconstitutional.

At the Tellings trial, 16 experts and others knowledgeable about dogs testified to the characteristics of pit bulls and statistics concerning dog bites as evidence of the danger of pit bulls to the public.[12] While the evidence was somewhat mixed, the majority of the evidence demonstrated that pit bulls are inherently no more dangerous than other breeds of dog.[13] In fact, the evidence suggested that pit bulls generally are loyal and loving family pets. The trial court found that the evidence did not prove that pit bulls were inherently more dangerous than other

---

8. *Tellings*, 2006 WL 513946, at *1.
9. Sentell v. New Orleans & C.R. Co., 166 U.S. 698, 705 (1897).
10. Hearn v. City of Overland Park, 772 P.2d 758, 765 (quoting Shadoan v. Barnett, 217 Ky. 205, 211 (1926)).
11. Nicchia v. New York, 254 U.S. 228, 230 (1920).
12. *Tellings*, 2006 WL 513946, at *1–2 .
13. *Id.* (Tellings presented 12 witnesses, while the state presented only four).

breeds of dogs but nevertheless held that they created a substantial threat to the public and found the statutes constitutional.[14]

Tellings appealed the trial court's decision and won. The Ohio Sixth Appellate District was persuaded by Tellings that the statute was unconstitutional on several grounds—vagueness, procedural and substantive due process, and equal protection.

Void for Vagueness

The statute in question in *Tellings* defined as "vicious" a dog "commonly known as a pit bull or pit bull mixed breed dog." A fundamental requirement of due process is for the law to provide adequate notice of what is required and to allow sufficient guidance to local authority in order to avoid arbitrary and discriminatory enforcement. The legal standard is quite low. The statute violates the constitution when it "leaves a reader of ordinary intelligence confused about the breadth of coverage."[15] The court stated that it was troubled by this statute's definition of the breed for several reasons. Most importantly, it lacked an exact definition since there is no breed of "pit bull."[16] In fact, at least ten breeds of non-pit bull dogs are easily confused with a dog "commonly known as a pit bull."[17] Moreover, given the greater number and variety of breeds of dogs defined in recent years, owners no longer can easily determine the breed of their dog.[18] Finally, given the lack of statutory guidance and varieties of breeds, the identification process is highly subjective and depends upon the zealousness and bias of local authority. Such determinations are based upon individual speculation as to whether the dog's jaw is massive enough, his chest muscular enough, or his brow broad enough.[19] Thus, the court found the statute unconstitutionally vague as there was no rational basis to positively identify a pit bull.

---

14. *Id.* at *5.
15. Am. Dog Owners v. Des Moines, 469 N.W.2d 416, 418 (Iowa 1991).
16. *Tellings*, 2006 WL 513946, at *12.
17. *Id.*
18. *Id.*
19. *Id.*

On appeal, the Ohio Supreme Court disagreed. In a terse quote from the 1991 *Anderson* decision, the court held: "The physical and behavioral traits of pit bulls together with commonly available knowledge of dog breeds typically acquired by potential dog owners or otherwise possessed by veterinarians or breeders are sufficient to inform a dog owner as to whether he owns a dog commonly known as a pit bull."[20] The court was unwilling to recognize the changes since 1991 in the breeding of dogs, including the increasing number and variety of dog breeds and the resulting difficulty in identifying breeds. Moreover, the court failed to appreciate the highly subjective nature of breed identification. Although mathematical precision is not required,[21] the evidence suggested that the identification of a dog commonly known as a pit bull provided little if any guidance.

Procedural Due Process

The essence of due process is timely notice of possible violation and a reasonable opportunity to be heard before being found in violation of a statute and sanctioned. When the state is acting pursuant to its police power, the process required depends upon the nature of the property, the necessity for its sacrifice, and the extent to which the requirements and regulations provided in the ordinance may be regarded as within the police power."[22]

Under the local statute at issue in *Tellings*, classification as a pit bull was an unrebuttable presumption of viciousness.[23] Moreover, the statute provided no opportunity for an owner to challenge the classification of a dog as a pit bull before being found in violation and sanctioned.[24] The appellate court held that this clearly violated the fundamental due process rights of owners because the owner had no opportunity to be heard before held in violation.[25] The appellate court relied on a recent Ohio Supreme Court case that had found the same statute unconsti-

---

20. *Tellings*, 871 N.E.2d at 1158 (quoting State v. Anderson, 77 Ohio St. 3d 168, 173 (1991)).
21. Vanater v. Village of S. Point, 717 F. Supp. 1236, 1244 (S.D. Ohio 1989).
22. *Sentell*, 166 U.S. at 705.
23. *Tellings*, 2006 WL 513946 at *7.
24. *Id.*
25. *Id.*

tutional for failure to provide for a hearing. In *Cowan*, the dog at issue had been determined to be vicious under a separate provision of the statute based on an alleged attack, rather than its breed.[26] The *Cowan* court held that an owner must be given an opportunity to challenge the finding of viciousness before being sanctioned. Since the statute failed to provide such an opportunity, the statute was unconstitutional.[27]

Surprisingly, the Ohio Supreme Court on appeal distinguished *Tellings* from *Cowan*, stating that unlike in *Cowan*, where the dog was determined to be vicious based on an alleged attack, determining that a dog is a pit bull, and thus vicious, does not mandate a hearing since "there is no concern about unilateral administrative decision-making on a case-by-case basis."[28] This holding is incredible and contradicts fundamental due process principles. The court assumed that the definition of a pit bull is clear and unambiguous and that the classification of a given dog is purely objective and thus a hearing is unnecessary. As the evidence at trial demonstrated and the appellate court held, neither is true.

Equal Protection and Substantive Due Process

The Ohio Sixth District was the first court to find that BSL violated the equal protection and substantive due process rights of pit bull owners as arbitrary, unreasonable, and irrational. The court first noted that while a dog is deemed property under the law, a special relationship exists between owners and their dogs. In fact, often a pet dog is as important and loved as human members of the family.[29] Nevertheless, the right to dog ownership is not a fundamental right. Moreover, classification based on breed of dog does not qualify as a suspect class under the equal protection clause as does "race" for humans. Thus, the statute can be both underinclusive (other breeds of dogs are dangerous) and overinclusive (many pit bulls are not dangerous) and be constitutional.[30] Under a rational basis standard of review, the law need only be

---

26. *Id.* at *6 (citing State v. Cowan, 103 Ohio St. 3d 144 (2004)).
27. *Id.*
28. *Tellings*, 871 N.E.2d at 1158.
29. *Tellings*, 2006 WL 513946, at *8.
30. Colo. Dog Fanciers v. Denver, 820 P.2d 644, 650 (Co. 1991).

rationally related to a legitimate government goal—generally the "kiss of death" for a finding of unconstitutionality. Nevertheless, there are some laws that have been found to be irrational and based purely on animus for the targeted group.[31] Interestingly, the appellate court found this statute to fall into that category.

It is clear that the goal of BSL is to protect the public, and this goal is clearly legitimate, if not compelling. The issue, however, is whether targeting specific breeds, such as pit bulls, is rationally related to achieving that goal. After reviewing the transcript of detailed evidence presented by numerous experts, the appellate court found that "most public opinions about this highly obedient, eager-to-please breed are not based on facts."[32] The evidence presented suggests that earlier cases upholding BSL were based on obsolete information that merely perpetuates an outdated stereotypical image of pit bulls as inherently vicious.[33] The court specifically noted that reliance on "bare statistics" of dog breeds involved in human fatalities, without referencing the total number of dogs in each breed population, has "no real relevance or meaning."[34] The court held that the regulation of a specific breed for reasons "unrelated to that breed, but rather related to human misconduct or negligence in ownership of the breed,"[35] is arbitrary, unreasonable, and discriminatory and thus irrational and unconstitutional. The court emphasized that this finding did not mean that owners were free to ignore their duty to protect others from their dogs. Indeed, it is unlawful to encourage a dog to be aggressive, use a dog for fighting, or permit the dog to behave in a threatening, dangerous, or vicious manner.[36] Nevertheless, this was the owners' responsibility independent of the breed of dog owned.

Unremarkably, the Ohio Supreme Court dismissed the appellate court's enlightened analysis swiftly stating that dogs are qualified property, and legislatures have broad police power to regulate dogs in order to protect the public.[37] The trial court had cited substantial evidence

31. *See, e.g.,* Romer v. Evans, 517 U.S. 620 (1996).
32. *Tellings,* 2006 WL 513946, at *3.
33. *Id.* at *10.
34. *Id.* at *4.
35. *Id.* at *11.
36. *Id.*
37. *Tellings,* 871 N.E.2d at 1158.

that pit bulls cause a disproportionate danger to the public,[38] thus the law is rationally related to a legitimate purpose. The Ohio Supreme Court failed to adequately address the reasoning of the appellate court in dismissing its analysis. The court was unwilling to evaluate the statistics and to account for new evidence concerning the temperament of pit bulls developed in the last two decades. Moreover, the court demonstrated no appreciation for the special relationship between owner and dog nor attributed the fundamental problem to reckless owners rather than the breed of the dog.

Privileges and Immunities; Takings

Tellings challenged the statute as an unconstitutional taking, but the appellate court did not discuss this ground as moot.[39] Moreover, other owners have challenged BSL under the Privilege and Immunities and Commerce clauses as well. These challenges have never been successful.

The takings argument is that seizing the dog based on breed is an abuse of power and thus an unconstitutional taking of private property without due compensation. Since dogs are "qualified" property, subject to the police power of the state, courts generally find no abuse of power as the seizure of the dog is rationally related to a legitimate government goal.[40] Since the appellate court in *Tellings* found the statute irrational, it could have held a takings violation as well, but settled on substantive due process and equal protection violations instead. Interestingly, this choice suggests that the court was loath to focus on the dog as merely property and thus subject to a takings challenge. Grounding the violation on more human-centric clauses signaled an appreciation for the dog as something more than mere property.

Under the privileges and immunities or commerce clauses, owners have tried to argue that the law infringes their right to travel by restricting the owners of pit bulls from outside the state to travel into the state. This argument has virtually no merit since states as independent

---

38. *Id.* at 1157.
39. Tellings, 2006 WL 513946, at *13.
40. *See, e.g.,* Colo. Dog Fanciers v. Denver, 820 P.2d 644, 653 (Co. 1991).

sovereigns have authority to regulate conduct within their state so long as they do it uniformly, treating residents and nonresidents alike.[41] Since BSLs limit pit bull ownership for everyone—residents and non-residents—there is no discrimination against nonresidents and thus no violation of the privileges and immunities or commerce clauses.[42]

Challenging BSL

Constitutional challenges to BSL generally have not fared well in court but, depending upon the law in a given jurisdiction, a challenge may succeed.

Vagueness

Vagueness challenges are the most common successful constitutional challenges of BSL. Unless the BSL in a jurisdiction defines a recognized breed by its formal name, such as American Pit Bull Terrier, American Staffordshire Terrier, and Staffordshire Terrier, one should challenge the definition as vague and thus providing insufficient notice to owners and insufficient guidance to local authority to accurately and fairly classify dogs under the definition. This in turn leads to arbitrary and discriminatory enforcement.[43]

Procedural Due Process

A procedural due process challenge may be successful if the law does not provide for adequate procedures to challenge the findings of the local authority. The cases have held that a preseizure hearing generally is not required, but a hearing before an unbiased fact finder prior to being held in violation of the law is necessary. Moreover, the owner must have adequate and timely notice and a reasonable opportunity to present evidence to challenge the findings of the authorities; thus an unrebuttable presumption that the dog is a pit bull and/or vicious

---

41. Califano v. Gautier Torres, 435 U.S. 1, 4 (1978).
42. *See, e.g.*, Bess v. Bracken County Fiscal Ct., 210 S.W.3d 177, 182–83 (Ky. 2006).
43. *See, e.g.*, Am. Dog Owners v. Des Moines, 469 N.W.2d at 416; Am. Dog Owners v. City of Lynn, 404 Mass. 73 (Ma. 1989).

is likely to be unconstitutional. Finally, if the burden of proof is on the owner of the dog rather than the locality or if the owner is limited in presenting evidence or cross-examining witnesses,[44] the court may find such a burden or limitation unconstitutional.

Equal Protection and Substantive Due Process

These challenges are unlikely to succeed unless the court is progressive and the evidence presented compelling. The key to success here is to demonstrate that the studies of dog behavior overwhelmingly prove that a dog's temperament is not related to its breed and that the "facts" that claim pit bulls as more dangerous than other dogs are not scientifically supported. With time and better research and study into dog behavior, these challenges may succeed. It is imperative to call expert witnesses in animal behavior and researchers who have conducted scientifically supported studies of dog temperament and the effectiveness of BSL to testify that BSL is ineffective and dog behavior is not a function of breed. For example, two European studies from Scotland[45] and Spain[46] have recently been published that compared dog-bite data before and after BSL was enacted. Both studies suggest that legislation targeting breeds was ineffective in reducing dog bites and that the targeted breeds accounted for very few reported bites.

Privileges and Immunities; Takings

No one has successfully challenged BSL on these grounds. The only statutes that may fall under one of these challenges are laws that either (1) prevent an owner from keeping a dog targeted by the law and owned at the time the statute is enacted and/or provide inadequate notice

---

44. *See, e.g.,* Bill Morlin, *Judge: Dog Ordinance Unconstitutional,* SPOKESMAN REVIEW (Spokane, Wash.), Dec. 2, 2007, *available at* http://www.spokesmanreview.com/breaking/story.asp?ID=12583 (law violated due process rights when owner unable to cross-examine or impeach witnesses involved in dog's impoundment).

45. B. Klaassen, J.R. Buckley & A. Esmail, *Does the Dangerous Dogs Act Protect Against Animal Attacks: A Prospective Study of Mammalian Bites in the Accident and Emergency Department,* 27(2) INJURY 89–91 (1996).

46. B. Rosado et al., *Spanish Dangerous Animals Act: Effect of the Epidemiology of Dog Bites,* 2(5) J. VET. BEHAVIOR 166–74 (2007).

and time to comply with the requirements of continued ownership or (2) discriminate between resident and nonresident dog owners.

In Conclusion: A Rational Concurrence

In 2006, the Ohio Sixth Appellate District appreciated how unfair and irrational it is to attempt to protect the public by targeting a breed of dog. Unfortunately its decision was short-lived and ultimately overturned. There was one bright spot in the Ohio Supreme Court's decision. Judge O'Connor of the Ohio Supreme Court concurred in the *Tellings* decision likely out of respect for the principal of separation of powers. While she chose not to substitute her judgment for that of the legislature, her words were quite moving and "telling." She concluded:

> Dangerous animal behavior is the function of inherently dangerous dog owners, not inherently dangerous dogs. . . . Because the danger posed by vicious dogs and pit bulls arises from the owner's failure to safely control the animal, rational legislation should focus on the owner of the dog rather than the specific breed that is owned.[47]

---

47. *Tellings*, 871 N.E.2d at 1159 (O'Connor, J., concurring in judgment only).

Part II

Enforcing and Defending Dangerous Dog Laws

Chapter 4

Prosecuting Dangerous Dog Cases

MICHELLE WELCH

Dangerous dog cases come in many breeds. The cases we have prosecuted include Dalmatians, golden retrievers, Labradors, pit bulls, Rottweilers, and even a Chihuahua. Any breed can become dangerous, because dangerous dogs become dangerous in one way: a "bad" owner. The owners either chained the dog incessantly or let them run free. Either way, the dogs are not to blame; the owners are.

Culpability of Owners

Dangerous dog cases are perhaps the hardest to prosecute because they typically become quite volatile, more so than animal cruelty cases. In fact, cruelty and neglect cases tend to be relatively simple to prosecute because one generally has horrendous evidence that is hard for the defendant to overcome. In those cases, a dog is dead because it has been starved to death or maimed because of the defendant's intentional cruel acts. In such cases, the defendant's culpability is seemingly evident. But in dangerous dog cases, the owners never think they are culpable, even though they are likely to be the real cause of the situation.

Dangerous dog cases can be divided into two classes: those with human victims and those with animal victims. The path of owner culpability is often easier to see in cases where a human has been maimed or killed. In one incident, a little girl had to have her arm sewn to her groin to regrow the skin that dogs had ripped from her. In that case, the owner had chained the dogs for their whole lives, and there was anecdotal evidence that the owner used them for dog fighting. The owner knew that the dogs, if unchained, could get out of the yard and that they had been a nuisance to the neighborhood in the past. On this fateful day, the owner left the dogs off chain, and a little girl suffered.

There is ample evidence that chaining causes psychological, emotional, and behavioral problems in dogs. It ruins the dogs' nature as social pack animals. Dogs that live out their lives on the end of chains become territorial and can become more aggressive. Such dogs are frustrated and will take out that frustration on other living beings. Media reports on dog attacks often portray the dog as a "family pet" that one day "inexplicably became dangerous"—but a dog living on the end of a chain 24 hours a day is not a family pet, and the temperament of a dog that has been chained incessantly is quite explicable.

In many instances when a dog attacks a human victim, the dogs have been chained and then somehow escape that chain. At the other end of the spectrum are dogs that are completely unrestrained and allowed to run in a pack, reinforcing their prey drive. Unrestrained dogs are frequently responsible for attacks on animal victims. The most egregious examples of this are dogs that habitually run at large, but also sometimes involve a family pet that gets out of the yard and attacks a cat or a smaller dog.

For example, a Labrador retriever and a Dalmatian that were running at large killed a neighborhood cat. The cat's owner wanted the dogs destroyed; the neighborhood was in agreement because the owner of the dogs was not sympathetic to the cat's owner and still allowed the dogs to run loose, controlling them by voice command alone. In the end, we resolved this case by allowing the owner to keep the Lab and to send the Dalmatian to live with a relative after obtaining permission from animal-control authorities in the new jurisdiction. The Dalmatian has done quite well in his new surroundings.

Are dogs that kill cats dangerous? The answer is arguable. On the one hand, some believe that animals that attack anything are "dangerous." However, others understand the instinct of a dog to attack another, smaller animal, and believe that this alone does not necessarily make the dog "dangerous." This, too, makes prosecuting these cases difficult.

At the center of all these cases is the owner. What an owner does and does not do affects the dog and, therefore, the public. An owner who chains a dog is making the dog aggressive. An owner who allows a dog to run at large may be allowing the dog to get into a situation where the dog is deemed dangerous because of its actions. Thus, the owner's actions are the ones that should and must be prosecuted.

In Virginia, the law now reflects the culpability of the owner (see Appendix 4-1). The law was changed in 2007 when Dorothy Sullivan died trying to save her small dog from being killed by dogs that were running at large. Until that time, although the offending dogs could be destroyed for maulings, the owner faced no real penalty. Additionally, the new law added a provision for a dangerous dog registry (see Appendix 4-2), now available on the Internet. If dangerous dog laws are to be effective, they must hold the owner responsible and not label any one breed dangerous. Any dog can be dangerous if cared for by a reckless owner. There is no constitutional right to own an animal; owning an animal is a privilege. That privilege comes with a duty to care for the animals under one's care.

Witnesses for the Prosecution

When prosecuting dangerous dog cases, the story must be told through witnesses—victims, eyewitnesses, animal control officers, forensic nurses, doctors, veterinarians, DNA experts—and other evidence, including photos or video of the scene, the offending dogs, and the victims' injuries. What follows are suggestions for handling witness testimony and other evidence.

Victim

First, elicit the victim's story. Ask him or her to describe what happened that day and identify the dog and dog owner. Ask what the dog was doing before the attack.

In most cases, identifying the dog is relatively easy. Sometimes the victim knows the dog and the dog owner. They may even be family friends. Frequently, someone breaks up the attack and can identify the accused dog. If not, animal control, if dispatched along with the police, may have caught the dog. If the victim cannot identify the dog, usually the animal control officer can. If the dog was not recovered, there is a dog DNA bank in California that may prove useful.

DNA evidence must be collected at time of the incident, or the evidence will be lost. Your local animal control department must be educated in the recovery of evidence such as saliva, hair, or dog blood from the victim's wounds so that they can educate others. Forensic nurses at your local emergency room should be well versed in the recovery of such evidence as well. Education is the key. The nurses or animal control officers may not know that there are labs that process dog DNA. In fact, your state lab may have this capability.

Also, circumstantial evidence often comes into play. The dog may have the victim's blood on it or a piece of the victim's clothing in its mouth. State labs may or may not have the resources to analyze the blood on the dog but should do so if necessary.

Animal Control or Police Officer

Law enforcement agents are professional and should be able to tell the story for you. Elicit in detail the scene that they witnessed. However, be careful that they do not start talking in "police" speak. Break down their testimony and ask for a lot of detail. The details are what will win the case for you. The animal control officer may be able to recount the history of the dog and its owner if there had been prior encounters. Officers will also have photos or video of the scene of the attack as well as photos of the dog. If the dog is highly aggressive, the officer may have video of the dog lunging on the catch pole or in its cage after being seized.

Make sure the officers have thoroughly investigated the case. They must ask the right questions of neighbors, including the frequency that the dog roamed at large, any evidence of dog fighting, any evidence of chaining, any evidence of animal aggression, any evidence of human aggression, any evidence linking the behavior of the animals to the owner's actions, and any evidence of the owner's knowledge of the behavior.

In the case of the little girl who was attacked, the owner knew the dogs could get out of the yard because the neighbors had told him repeatedly that they were getting out. Despite all those warnings, he let them off chain the day they attacked the little girl. Neighbors had also witnessed the owner separating the dogs when they were attacking each other. Further, although the neighbors had also told animal control that the owner had fought the dogs, they would not testify to that on the stand.

Neighbors and Other Witnesses

A prosecutor, investigator, or animal control officer should canvas the neighborhood to seek other witnesses. Elicit the history of the animals from the neighborhood witnesses. Find out what they know, including the frequency that the dog roamed at large, any evidence of dog fighting, any evidence of chaining, any evidence of animal aggression, any evidence of human aggression, and any evidence linking the behavior of the dog to the owner. In the case of the little girl, a neighbor who was working on the roof of a house had seen the owner pry the dogs apart from fighting each other. Of course, one problem with neighborhood witnesses is getting them to show up and testify. However, if you explain the need for their testimony to help resolve the problem in their neighborhood, you may persuade them to testify.

Forensic Nurses

Although forensic nurses may or may not get involved in a dog-bite case, you should generally call them in a more-serious case of mauling. It is particularly necessary for them to collect evidence for the lab in a case in which the dog is not known. As they may just focus on documenting the extent of the wounds for the court, it is important to educate forensic nurses on these cases and how to collect the evidence of dog blood, saliva, or hair from the victim's wounds.

Forensic nurses are marvelous witnesses because they often get statements from the victim that the victim may not remember later. It certainly helps you prep the victim for court when you can refer to what the victim reported the day of the incident.

You also will get a lot of your documentary evidence from forensic nurses. They take many photos of the wounds from all directions and write an extremely detailed report on the condition of the victim.

Treating Physicians

If the forensic nurse does not follow the victim through recovery, you may also have to call the treating physician. In the case of a mauling, the doctor will tell the story of how the victim recovered. In the case of the little girl who was mauled so badly her hand was sewn to her groin for weeks, the doctor was invaluable in testifying as to how many surgeries the girl had to go through (more than 12) and her prognosis for the future.

Doctors can also testify in dangerous dog cases where there is a single dog bite. You should elicit testimony from the doctor regarding the seriousness of the bite and the treatment. You may or may not want to admit the doctor's notes into evidence. Be certain to obtain any photos the doctor has and admit them into evidence through the doctor. If the case is a criminal case, the doctor must testify because affidavits and depositions are not admissible. Moreover, the doctor's report can be admitted only if the doctor testifies.

Veterinarian or State Veterinarian

Veterinarians testify frequently in animal cruelty cases and sometimes in dangerous dog cases as well. Most dangerous dog cases are not sent to the state veterinarian, but a local veterinarian often gets involved. The veterinarian may have examined the accused dog or may have treated an animal victim. You should obtain the veterinarian's report and photos and admit them into evidence through the veterinarian's testimony. If the victim animal lives, you will want to have the veterinarian testify to the extent of the animal's injuries and necessary treatment.

Animal Behaviorist

It may be relevant to call an animal behaviorist to testify about the behavior of the dog, especially if the dog was temperament-tested either in the past or upon seizure. If you can qualify the animal behaviorist as an expert, the witness may also testify to the natural instinct of the dog under the specific situation.

DNA Expert

The need to call a dog DNA expert is rare because usually the officer has caught the animal in question. But there may be a case in which the identity of the perpetrating dog is unclear; for example, if more than one dog is present when a person is mauled. As discussed above, the evidence must be collected at the time of the incident, generally by the forensic nurse. To accomplish this, the animal control officer or police officer must communicate with emergency personnel to request that they collect such evidence and follow up the request at the hospital and with the forensic nurse. If the evidence is collected, then the DNA expert can testify to the identity of the dog.

Remember, chain of custody must be maintained. DNA is complex and it is imperative that you as a prosecutor educate yourself by talking with the DNA expert. You must qualify the expert as an expert in dog DNA and then have the report admitted. Some state labs have the capability to determine dog DNA, others do not. The Canine Health Information Center has partnered with the University of California at Davis and the University of Missouri to develop and maintain a Dog DNA Repository.[1] This repository may also aid your investigation.

Conclusion

The new Virginia law, though still a work in progress, now addresses the responsibility and the culpability of the owner. In most cases, the owner bears most, if not all, of the blame for a dog's actions. More-

---

1. Canine Health Information DNA Repository at http://www.caninehealthinfo.org/dnabank.html.

over, the dangerous dog registry, while not perfect, is the first in the nation to allow jurisdictions to track problem dogs from jurisdiction to jurisdiction. Prosecuting dangerous dog cases can be difficult but is necessary. Hopefully these suggestions will aid the prosecution of your cases.

Appendix 4-1

Virginia's Dangerous Dog Law

(Va. Code Ann. § 3.1-796.93:1 (2007))

TITLE 3.1.   AGRICULTURE, HORTICULTURE AND FOOD
CHAPTER 27.4.   COMPREHENSIVE ANIMAL LAWS
ARTICLE 4.   AUTHORITY OF LOCAL GOVERNING BODIES
                  AND LICENSING OF DOGS

§ 3.1-796.93:1. Control of dangerous or vicious dogs; penalties

A. As used in this section:

"Dangerous dog" means a canine or canine crossbreed that has bitten, attacked, or inflicted injury on a person or companion animal that is a dog or cat, or killed a companion animal that is a dog or cat. However, when a dog attacks or bites a companion animal that is a dog or cat, the attacking or biting dog shall not be deemed dangerous (i) if no serious physical injury as determined by a licensed veterinarian has occurred to the dog or cat as a result of the attack or bite, (ii) if both animals are owned by the same person, (iii) if such attack occurs on the property of the attacking or biting dog's owner or custodian, or (iv) for other good cause as determined by the court. No dog shall be found to be a dangerous dog as a result of biting, attacking, or inflicting injury on a dog or cat while engaged with an owner or custodian as part of lawful hunting or participating in an organized, lawful dog handling event.

"Vicious dog" means a canine or canine crossbreed that has (i) killed a person; (ii) inflicted serious injury to a person, including multiple bites, serious disfigurement, serious impairment of health, or serious impairment of a bodily function; or (iii) continued to exhibit the behavior that resulted in a previous finding by a court or, on or before July 1, 2006, by an animal control officer as authorized by local ordinance, that it is a dangerous dog, provided that its owner has been given notice of that finding.

B. Any law-enforcement officer or animal control officer who has reason to believe that a canine or canine crossbreed within his

jurisdiction is a dangerous dog or vicious dog shall apply to a magis-
trate of the jurisdiction for the issuance of a summons requiring the
owner or custodian, if known, to appear before a general district court
at a specified time. The summons shall advise the owner of the nature
of the proceeding and the matters at issue. If a law-enforcement officer
successfully makes an application for the issuance of a summons, he
shall contact the local animal control officer and inform him of the
location of the dog and the relevant facts pertaining to his belief that
the dog is dangerous or vicious. The animal control officer shall confine the animal until such time as evidence shall be heard and a verdict
rendered. If the animal control officer determines that the owner or
custodian can confine the animal in a manner that protects the public
safety, he may permit the owner or custodian to confine the animal
until such time as evidence shall be heard and a verdict rendered. The
court, through its contempt powers, may compel the owner, custodian
or harborer of the animal to produce the animal. If, after hearing the
evidence, the court finds that the animal is a dangerous dog, the court
shall order the animal's owner to comply with the provisions of this
section. If, after hearing the evidence, the court finds that the animal
is a vicious dog, the court shall order the animal euthanized in accor-
dance with the provisions of § 3.1-796.119. The procedure for appeal
and trial shall be the same as provided by law for misdemeanors. Trial
by jury shall be as provided in Article 4 (§ 19.2-260 et seq.) of Chapter
15 of Title 19.2. The Commonwealth shall be required to prove its case
beyond a reasonable doubt.

C. No canine or canine crossbreed shall be found to be a dangerous dog or vicious dog solely because it is a particular breed, nor is the
ownership of a particular breed of canine or canine crossbreed prohibited. No animal shall be found to be a dangerous dog or vicious
dog if the threat, injury or damage was sustained by a person who was
(i) committing, at the time, a crime upon the premises occupied by
the animal's owner or custodian, (ii) committing, at the time, a willful
trespass upon the premises occupied by the animal's owner or custodian, or (iii) provoking, tormenting, or physically abusing the animal,
or can be shown to have repeatedly provoked, tormented, abused, or
assaulted the animal at other times. No police dog that was engaged in

the performance of its duties as such at the time of the acts complained of shall be found to be a dangerous dog or a vicious dog. No animal that, at the time of the acts complained of, was responding to pain or injury, or was protecting itself, its kennel, its offspring, a person, or its owner's or custodian's property, shall be found to be a dangerous dog or a vicious dog.

D. If the owner of an animal found to be a dangerous dog is a minor, the custodial parent or legal guardian shall be responsible for complying with all requirements of this section.

E. The owner of any animal found to be a dangerous dog shall, within 10 days of such finding, obtain a dangerous dog registration certificate from the local animal control officer or treasurer for a fee of $ 50, in addition to other fees that may be authorized by law. The local animal control officer or treasurer shall also provide the owner with a uniformly designed tag that identifies the animal as a dangerous dog. The owner shall affix the tag to the animal's collar and ensure that the animal wears the collar and tag at all times. All certificates obtained pursuant to this subsection shall be renewed annually for the same fee and in the same manner as the initial certificate was obtained. The animal control officer shall provide a copy of the dangerous dog registration certificate and verification of compliance to the State Veterinarian.

F. All dangerous dog registration certificates or renewals thereof required to be obtained under this section shall only be issued to persons 18 years of age or older who present satisfactory evidence (i) of the animal's current rabies vaccination, if applicable, (ii) that the animal has been neutered or spayed, and (iii) that the animal is and will be confined in a proper enclosure or is and will be confined inside the owner's residence or is and will be muzzled and confined in the owner's fenced-in yard until the proper enclosure is constructed. In addition, owners who apply for certificates or renewals thereof under this section shall not be issued a certificate or renewal thereof unless they present satisfactory evidence that (i) their residence is and will continue to be posted with clearly visible signs warning both minors and adults of the presence of a dangerous dog on the property and (ii) the animal has been permanently identified by means of a tattoo on the inside thigh or by electronic implantation. All certificates or renewals thereof required to be obtained under this section shall only be issued to persons who present satisfactory evidence that the owner has liability insurance coverage, to the value of at least $ 100,000, that covers animal bites. The owner may obtain and maintain a bond in surety, in lieu of liability insurance, to the value of at least $ 100,000.

G. While on the property of its owner, an animal found to be a dangerous dog shall be confined indoors or in a securely enclosed and locked structure of sufficient height and design to prevent its escape or direct contact with or entry by minors, adults, or other animals. The structure shall be designed to provide the animal with shelter from the elements of nature. When off its owner's property, an animal found to be a dangerous dog shall be kept on a leash and muzzled in such a manner as not to cause injury to the animal or interfere with the animal's vision or respiration, but so as to prevent it from biting a person or another animal.

H. The owner of any dog found to be dangerous shall register the animal with the Commonwealth of Virginia Dangerous Dog Registry, as established under § 3.1-796.93:3, within 45 days of such a finding by a court of competent jurisdiction.

The owner shall also cause the local animal control officer to be promptly notified of (i) the names, addresses, and telephone numbers of all owners; (ii) all of the means necessary to locate the owner and the dog at any time; (iii) any complaints or incidents of attack by the dog upon any person or cat or dog; (iv) any claims made or lawsuits brought as a result of any attack; (v) tattoo or chip identification information or both; (vi) proof of insurance or surety bond; and (vii) the death of the dog.

I. After an animal has been found to be a dangerous dog, the animal's owner shall immediately, upon learning of same, cause the local animal control authority to be notified if the animal (i) is loose or unconfined; or (ii) bites a person or attacks another animal; or (iii) is sold, given away, or dies. Any owner of a dangerous dog who relocates to a new address shall, within 10 days of relocating, provide written notice to the appropriate local animal control authority for the old address from which the animal has moved and the new address to which the animal has been moved.

J. Any owner or custodian of a canine or canine crossbreed or other animal is guilty of a:

1. Class 2 misdemeanor if the canine or canine crossbreed previously declared a dangerous dog pursuant to this section, when such declaration arose out of a separate and distinct incident, attacks and injures or kills a cat or dog that is a companion animal belonging to another person;

2. Class 1 misdemeanor if the canine or canine crossbreed previously declared a dangerous dog pursuant to this section, when such declaration arose out of a separate and distinct incident, bites a human being or attacks a human being causing bodily injury; or

3. Class 6 felony if any owner or custodian whose willful act or omission in the care, control, or containment of a canine, canine crossbreed, or other animal is so gross, wanton, and culpable as to show a reckless disregard for human life, and is the proximate cause of such dog or other animal attacking and causing serious bodily injury to any person.

The provisions of this subsection shall not apply to any animal that, at the time of the acts complained of, was responding to pain or injury, or was protecting itself, its kennel, its offspring, a person, or its owner's or custodian's property, or when the animal is a police dog that is engaged in the performance of its duties at the time of the attack.

K. The owner of any animal that has been found to be a dangerous dog who willfully fails to comply with the requirements of this section is guilty of a Class 1 misdemeanor.

L. All fees collected pursuant to this section, less the costs incurred by the animal control authority in producing and distributing the certificates and tags required by this section, shall be paid into a special dedicated fund in the treasury of the locality for the purpose of paying the expenses of any training course required under § 3.1-796.104:1.

M. The governing body of any locality may enact an ordinance parallel to this statute regulating dangerous and vicious dogs; provided, however, that no locality may impose a felony penalty for violation of such local ordinances.

§ 3.1-796.93:3. Establishment of Dangerous Dog Registry.

The Commissioner shall establish the Commonwealth of Virginia Dangerous Dog Registry to be maintained by the Virginia Department of Agriculture and Consumer Services, Office of Veterinary Services. Each owner of any canine or canine crossbreed found by any court of competent jurisdiction to be a dangerous dog shall be required to register the animal as a dangerous dog within 45 days of such finding. The State Veterinarian shall receive, post, and maintain the information provided by the owner, animal control officers, and other such officials statewide on a website. All information collected for the Dangerous Dog Registry shall be available to animal control officers via the website. Registration shall include the name of the animal, a photograph, sex, age, weight, primary breed, secondary breed, color and markings, whether spayed or neutered, the acts that resulted in the dog being designated as dangerous and associated trial docket information, microchip or tattoo number, address where the animal is maintained, name of the owner, address of the owner, telephone numbers of the owner, and a statement that the owner has complied with the provisions of the dangerous dog order. The address of the owner along with the name and breed of the dangerous dog, the acts that resulted in the dog being deemed dangerous, and information necessary to access court records of the adjudication shall be available to the general public. By January 31 of each year, until such time as the dangerous dog is deceased, the owner shall submit a renewal registration that shall include all information contained in the original registration and any updates. The owner shall verify the information is accurate by annual resubmissions. The owner shall submit to the State Veterinarian a $100 initial registration fee and a $35 renewal registration fee. In the event that the dangerous dog is moved to a different location, or contact information for the owner changes in any way at any time, the owner shall submit a renewal containing the address of the new location or other updated information within 10 days of such move or change. There shall be no charge for any updated information provided between renewals.

Any funds collected pursuant to this section shall be used by the State Veterinarian to maintain the registry and website. The website list shall be known as the Virginia Dangerous Dog Registry. Actions of the Department relating to the establishment, operation, and maintenance of the Commonwealth of Virginia Dangerous Dog Registry under this section shall be exempt from the provisions of the Administrative Process Act (§ 2.2-4000 et seq.).

Appendix 4-2
Virginia's Dangerous Dog Registry

Virginia's dangerous dog registry provides owner name and information and the dog's name along with the telephone number of animal control to report any problems with the dog.

Initially, the Virginia Department of Agriculture and Consumer Services (VDACS), which administers the online registry, posted more information than necessary. The listing now contains only information available in the court records, which are public records.

Only owners convicted of the dangerous dog law are placed on the registry. VDACS lists breed information and summarizes the reasons that a dog was declared dangerous. It also names the animal control officer who made the arrest.

All dogs that had been declared dangerous prior to the law changing in 2007 are placed on the registry, but they do not necessarily have to comply with all the requirements of the new law. The registry details whether the owners must comply with the requirements of insurance under the new law.

The responsibility for collecting the data now lies with local animal control organizations. The animal control officers enter the data and then VDACS approves it before it appears on the website. The Dangerous Dog Registry does not include vicious dogs, defined as those who mauled a person severely, because under Virginia law, vicious dogs are euthanized. Many breeds are represented on the registry. Some localities do not list any dangerous dogs at all; examples from localities that do list dangerous dogs follow.

City of Richmond: Dangerous Dog # 0641

Main Animal Control Contact Number
If you need to report an issue with this dog, call **804-646-5573**

Summary Information
Owner—Phyllis A Christian

Dog—Gabby
1107 North 23rd Street
Richmond, VA 23223

Dog Information
Name of Dangerous Dog: Gabby
Primary Breed: American Pit Bull
Secondary Breed: none
Color and Markings: Tan/White

Trial Docket Info
Acts resulting in the dog being declared dangerous: Dog bit owner.
Docket Number: GC04009895-00
Parties: Christian, Phyllis
Court: Richmond General District / Criminal (North)
Judge: Henderson
Adjudication Date: 11/04/04
Requirements imposed on owner by judge: Prior to Dangerous Dog
Law; owner does not have to obtain liability insurance or bond.

Animal Control Officer Info
Keegan Merrick
1600 Chamberlayne Avenue
Richmond, VA 23222
Phone Number(s): 804-646-5573

City of Newport News: Dangerous Dog # Unassigned
Main Animal Control Contact Number
If you need to report an issue with this dog, call **757-595-7387**

Summary Information
Owner—Shawn Cobb
Dog—Bear
27 Ridgewood Parkway
Newport News, VA 23608

Dog Information
Name of Dangerous Dog: Bear
Primary Breed: Labrador
Secondary Breed: Golden Retriever
Color and Markings: Yellow

Trial Docket Info
Acts resulting in the dog being declared dangerous: Dog bit woman on the back of the leg as she rode by on her bike
Docket Number: 700CR06c36618-00
Parties: Newport News vs Shawn Cobb
Court: Newport News Circuit Court
Judge: Judge Pugh
Adjudication Date: 01/18/07
Requirements imposed on owner by judge: N/A

Animal Control Officer Info
Christine Riley
9287 Warwick Blvd
Newport News, VA 23607
Phone Number(s): 757-595-7387

City of Newport News: Dangerous Dog # 0876

Main Animal Control Contact Number
If you need to report an issue with this dog, call **757-595-7387**

Summary Information
Owner—John Ladusky III
Dog—Randy
3 Paula Dr
Newport News, VA 23608

Dog Information
Name of Dangerous Dog: Randy
Primary Breed: German Shepherd

Secondary Breed: none
Color and Markings: Black and Tan

Trial Docket Info
Acts resulting in the dog being declared dangerous: Dog's head came over victim's fence and bit victim on the back.
Docket Number: GC06011108-00
Parties: Elpidio Manoso
Court: General District/Criminal
Judge: unknown
Adjudication Date: 12/13/06
Requirements imposed on owner by judge: N/A

Animal Control Officer Info
Atiya Pope
9287 Warwick Blvd
Newport News, VA 23607
Phone Number(s): 757-595-7387

York County: Dangerous Dog # 0566

Main Animal Control Contact Number
If you need to report an issue with this dog, call 757-890-3600

Summary Information
Owner—Lori A Shields
Dog—Angel
107 Heritage Place
Yorktown, VA 23690

Dog Information
Name of Dangerous Dog: Angel
Primary Breed: Chesapeake bay ret
Secondary Breed: None
Color and Markings: Brown

Trial Docket Info
Acts resulting in the dog being declared dangerous: Carlyn Turpin was at 106 Heritage pl when angel ran up to her and bit her on the arm and leg. Ruby Walker was approached by three dogs from 107 Heritage Pl and was scratched on the back by angel. Mr Caragianis was bit in the face and required surgery.
Docket Number: GC0300808300
Parties: Mr & Mrs Shields, Mrs Walker, Mrs Turpin, Mr Caragianis
Court: York County
Judge: Judge Renne
Adjudication Date: 09/30/03
Requirements imposed on owner by judge: To comply with York County DANGEROUS DOG CODE4-37

Animal Control Officer Info
Mitch D Monroe
P O Box 532
Yorktown, VA 23690
Phone Number(s): 757-890-3601; 757-897-1874

Chapter 5

Defending Allegedly Dangerous Dogs: The Florida Experience

MARCY LAHART

Introduction

Animal control officials must strike a delicate balancing in dealing with dogs that have been involved in an incident of aggression against a human or another animal. If the offending dog is truly aggressive and the animal control agency fails to act, the agency will certainly be blamed, and maybe even sued if another such incident occurs.[1] However, if the agency is heavy-handed it may face public outcry and ultimately be civilly liable for wrongly confiscating or killing someone's beloved family pet.[2]

There are some dogs that because of poor breeding or irresponsible owners, or both, are a legitimate risk to public health and safety. In a perfect world those dogs would not have to be killed but would be sent to a "nice home in the country" where they could be rehabilitated or live out their lives without posing a threat to people or to other animals. However, the reality is that animal shelters in the United States kill millions of unwanted dogs every year, most of which would never harm anyone or anything.

---

1. *See* Carter v. City of Stuart, 468 So. 2d 995 (Fla. 1985), in which the Florida Supreme Court held that despite an allegation that the city failed to enforce its animal control ordinance, the city was not liable for damages suffered when a dog that had escaped its confinement on private property attacked and severely injured a minor child. The court left open the door for such liability by refusing to conclude that there were no circumstances under which a governmental unit may be subjected to liability for the failure to enforce its laws.

2. *See, e.g.*, Altman v. City of High Point, N.C., 330 F.3d 194, 205 (4th Cir. 2003).

The resources for rehabilitating or safely housing canine criminals just do not exist, and the government's authority to seize and destroy dogs has been routinely upheld. For example, although speaking *in dictum*, the U.S. Supreme Court recognized the power of the state to require destruction of dogs as long ago as 1897.[3] However, case law recognizing that people have a property interest in their dogs, and requiring notice before a dog can be destroyed, dates back almost as far.[4]

It is a difficult task to enact regulations that allow animal control officials sufficient authority and flexibility to protect the public from truly dangerous dogs while also protecting dogs and their owners from arbitrary or unduly harsh actions of those officials. Many of the current laws and ordinances that govern the supposedly "dangerous" or "vicious" dogs are overly broad, allowing a dog to be muzzled or killed for simply engaging in normal dog behavior that is in no way a real indicator of aggressive tendencies towards humans or other animals.

For example, under the Florida dangerous dog statute a dog can be declared dangerous if it has, when unprovoked, "chased or approached a person upon the streets, sidewalks, or any public grounds in a menacing fashion or apparent attitude of attack."[5] Standards such as "menacing fashion" or "apparent attitude of attack" are hardly examples of legislative clarity. This provision could allow a dog to be declared dangerous simply for barking at a stranger while in a park.

Some current dangerous dog laws also leave far too much discretion in the hands of animal control officers, who may have little understanding of canine behavior or have a personal ax to grind with a particular dog, dog owner, or breed of dog. The City of Port St. Lucie, Florida, has an ordinance that allows a dog to be declared dangerous if the dog "has, in the opinion of an Animal Control Officer or law enforcement officer, posed a threat to the safety and welfare of the

---

3. *Sentell v. New Orleans & C. R. Co.*, 166 U.S. 698 (1897).

4. *Rose v. Salem*, 77 Or. 77 (Or. 1915). Under Oregon law it was larceny to steal a dog since dogs were expressly declared by statute to be personal property. The court said that whatever the law might be in other jurisdictions, in Oregon dogs were regarded as being just as important a class of personal property as other domestic animals and equally entitled to the protection of the law. Therefore, an ordinance providing for the summary destruction of animals without a judicial hearing and without actual or constructive notice to the owner was void.

5. Fla. Stat. § 767.11(1)(d).

community."[6] There is no requirement that the "opinion" that the dog "posed a threat to the safety and welfare of the community" be based upon the dog having injured or even threatened another animal or a person, or that an animal control or law enforcement officer have even the most rudimentary understanding of animal behavior.

Moreover, while defending a dog facing destruction or characterization as "dangerous" is challenging, there are certain actions that an attorney should take to provide the best defense possible for the dog and its owner.

Due Process

To address substantive and procedural due process concerns, a dangerous dog regulation should specify minimum findings that must be made before a dog is either subject to more onerous manner of keeping restrictions, or destroyed. Further, the regulation should provide for a full and fair hearing in front of an impartial decision-maker according to published procedural rules that inform concerned parties regarding standard of proof, burden of proof, evidentiary standards, process for compelling witnesses, and perhaps most important, who has the obligation to preserve the record of the hearing for appeal.

Substantive Due Process and the Curious Case of Cody

Cody is a German shepherd who lives with his owner, Charles Henshall, in Volusia County in Central Florida. Henshall owns a moving business, and sometimes stores clients' belongings during the moving process. Thus Cody lived with Henshall at the headquarters of the moving company, both as a companion and to protect the property and warn of intruders.

At the request of an employee whose nephew was looking for temporary work, Henshall allowed the 17-year-old nephew to work on the premises, but warned him not to enter the office without knocking first because of Cody. Later that morning the nephew entered the

---

6. City of Port St. Lucie Code of Ordinances 92.02(a)(1)(b)(2),

office without knocking despite the previous admonition and numerous "bad dog" signs. Unfortunately, his unannounced entry occurred just as Henshall's assistant returned through the back door from a walk with Cody and, unaware of the nephew's presence, let Cody off his leash. Cody charged into the front office and grabbed the nephew by the leg, shaking it back and forth. Cody lost his grip and then bit down a second time, and for that second bite he received a death sentence from the County's animal control board.

Florida's dangerous dog law, Chapter 767, establishes a procedure by which a dog may be declared dangerous, and thus subject to stringent manner of keeping requirements. A dog that has been formally declared "dangerous" must be registered as such with the appropriate animal control agency, must be kept inside "or in a securely enclosed and locked pen or structure, suitable to prevent the entry of young children and designed to prevent the animal from escaping. Such pen or structure shall have secure sides and a secure top to prevent the dog from escaping over, under, or through the structure and shall also provide protection from the elements."[7] A "dangerous" dog can be off the owner's property only if muzzled and "restrained by a substantial chain or leash and under control of a competent person."[8] Additionally, the owner of a "dangerous" dog must inform the animal control authority if the dog is moved to a new location, if the dog gets loose or bites someone, and if the dog is given away or dies.[9]

The Volusia County Animal Control Board did not consider whether or not Cody should be declared a dangerous dog. Instead, they concluded that Cody must be killed under the statute, which states in relevant part that "[i]f a dog that has not been declared dangerous attacks and *causes severe injury* to or death of any human, the dog shall be immediately confiscated by an animal control authority, placed in quarantine, if necessary, for the proper length of time or held for 10 business days after the owner is given written notification . . . and thereafter destroyed in an expeditious and humane manner."[10] Because

7. FLA. STAT. § 767.11(4) (2009).
8. *Id.* § 767.12(1)(b)
9. *Id.* § 767.12.
10. *Id.* § 767. 13(2) (emphasis added).

the statutory definition of severe injury includes "multiple bites"[11] and because Cody had lost his grip on the victim's leg and then clamped down a second time, the members of the animal control board concluded that they had no alternative but to order Cody destroyed without consideration of mitigating circumstances. Accordingly, the board did not wish to hear about the relatively minor nature of the wounds[12] or about the fact that the bite victim walked past bad dog signs and ignored a prior warning to not enter the office without knocking. Had the County instead declared Cody "dangerous," meaning subject to more stringent manner of keeping requirements, a host of defenses could have been raised.[13]

On appeal, the court found that the statute deprived dog owners of substantive due process[14] because it failed to consider the circumstances surrounding a dog that had bitten and caused "severe injury." The judge stated that the government had a legitimate interest not in regulating dogs that bite, but in regulating dogs that bite without provocation. Accordingly, Cody was eventually returned to his owner, but not after a lengthy and expensive stay in the quarantine area of the local humane society while the appeal was briefed and decided. A subsequent case against Volusia County for depriving Henshall of his

11. "Severe injury" means any physical injury that results in broken bones, multiple bites, or disfiguring lacerations requiring sutures or reconstructive surgery. *Id.* § 767.11(3).

12. When questioned concerning the extent of any lasting effects of the injury, the victim replied, "I couldn't go to no Halloween parties I wanted to go to. My friends wanted to go to places, I couldn't go with them."

13. A dog shall not be declared dangerous if the threat, injury, or damage was sustained by a person who, at the time, was unlawfully on the property or, while lawfully on the property, was tormenting, abusing, or assaulting the dog or its owner or a family member. No dog may be declared dangerous if the dog was protecting or defending a human being within the immediate vicinity of the dog from an unjustified attack or assault.

14. The test applied to determine whether or not a statute violates the substantive due process provision of Article 1, Section 9 of the Florida Constitution is "whether it bears a reasonable relation to a permissible legislative objective and is not discriminatory, arbitrary or oppressive." Lasky v. State Farm Ins. Co., 296 So. 2d 9, 15 (Fla. 1974); *see also* Young v. Broward County, 570 So. 2d 309 (Fla. Dist. Ct. App 1990) (Substantive due process test is whether the state can justify infringement of its legislative activity upon personal rights and liberties; statute must bear reasonable relationship to legislative objective and not be arbitrary.).

property, Cody, under color of an unconstitutional state statute[15] was settled out of court.

Procedural Due Process for Liner

Under the 14th Amendment to the United States Constitution, "no person shall be deprived of life, liberty, or property without due process of the law." Dogs are property under the law, and accordingly a dog's owner has a protected property right in his or her dog, which may not be deprived except in accord with all of the elements of due process.[16]

The extent of due process required in a particular matter varies with the character of the interest and the nature of the proceeding involved. The determination of what due process protections apply requires consideration of three factors: (1) the private interest that will be affected by the official action; (2) the risk of erroneous deprivation of such interest through the procedures used, and the probable value of additional or substitute procedural safeguards; and (3) the government's interest.[17]

Liner is a large pit bull–type dog who was sentenced to death by the City of St. Lucie Animal Control even though he had never bitten a person, nor was there any eyewitness evidence that he had attacked another animal. The City of Port St Lucie had adopted its own ordinance to supplement the Florida state dangerous dog law, Chapter 767. Under the city ordinance, an animal control officer could designate a dog "vicious," subjecting it to a host of additional restrictions that mirror the restrictions placed on a dog formally declared dangerous under the state law.[18] A "vicious" dog is subject to confinement in a special enclosure, must be on a leash and muzzled if off the owner's property, and be registered as a "vicious dog" with the city animal control, which was to be notified if the dog was ever taken to a location other than the

---

15. 42 U.S.C. § 1983 (2009).

16. Pasco v. Reihl, 620 So. 2d 229 (1st Fla. Dist. Ct. App. 1993), aff'd, 635 So. 2d 229 (Fla. 1994)

17. Mathews v. Eldridge, 424 U.S. 319 (1976).

18. At the time of Liner's seizure, City of Port St. Lucie Code of Ordinances 92.01 defined a "vicious animal" as "any animal(s) of fierce or dangerous propensities which is likely to cause or has caused injury to a person or damage to property, or any animal(s) which exhibit traits which are ungovernable or has a history of unprovoked attacks to any person(s) or animal(s)."

owner's home. Under the City's ordinance, if the owner of a "vicious" dog was more than once not in compliance with the manner of keeping restrictions, the dog could be seized and destroyed, regardless of whether the dog had caused any harm.

Liner's trouble began when he escaped from his owner's backyard along with his father, Boss, another pit bull–type dog. Animal control, responding to a call that the dogs were at large, arrived to find the dogs tied to a tree. Both dogs had puncture wounds, so the City, concluding that the dogs must have been fighting, destroyed Boss, who had been declared "vicious" based upon a previous incident, and declared Liner "vicious." Liner's owner was given a list of restrictions that applied to Liner, and, according to animal control officials, was verbally told that he could ask for a hearing. However, he was not provided written notice of a right to request a hearing, and the ordinance itself does not provide for a hearing regarding whether a dog should be declared "vicious."

Liner was again out of his yard some months later, but was sitting peacefully at his own front door when he was impounded by animal control without incident. Liner's third brush with the law came when he bolted out of an open warehouse and barked at a woman pedaling by on a bicycle. The woman was not injured, and did not immediately report the incident, but called police later. Animal control came and seized Liner and informed his owner that because he had twice violated the City's vicious dog ordinance, Liner would be destroyed. Although the ordinance did not expressly provide for a hearing, the owner requested and was granted a hearing before a special master, at which animal control's decision to destroy the "vicious dog" for not being in compliance with the manner of keeping restrictions was upheld.

However, it is long established that gratuitous hearings do not satisfy due process concerns; rather, a law that deprives someone of property must explicitly allow for a hearing.[19] In reversing a death penalty determination for a female Labrador that had been ordered destroyed subsequent to a hearing, the California Court of Appeal observed,

> A hearing granted as a matter of discretion is no substitute for due process. It is not enough that the owners may by chance have notice,

---

19. Coe v. Armour Fertilizer Works, 237 U.S. 413 (1915).

or that they may as a matter of favor have a hearing. The law must require notice to them, and give them the right to a hearing and an opportunity to be heard. It is irrelevant that the question may have been fairly decided by a courtesy hearing or that the plaintiff lacks a defense on the merits. The rule is well settled that to constitute due process of law in regard to the taking of property the statute should give the parties interested some adequate remedy for the vindication of their rights. A provision in the statute or ordinance providing a hearing ensures that the response of the administrative entity will be a settled and uniform, and not an [sic] haphazard, procedure.[20]

Two appeals later, the circuit court finally sided with Liner and his owner and held that the City of Port St. Lucie ordinance was unconstitutional because it did not provide for a hearing regarding whether a dog should be declared vicious. Thus, the statute violated dog owners' right to procedural due process.[21]

Similarly, other dangerous dog regulations have been found to violate due process requirements based upon other infirmities. For example, in *Mansour v. King County*,[22] the court found that King County's lack of a clearly ascertainable standard of proof, as well as the inability to subpoena witnesses and records, violated the procedural due process rights of a pet owner ordered to remove his pet from the county or give her up to be euthanized.

Defending a Dog at a Dangerous Dog Hearing

Dangerous dog hearings are difficult to win at the "trial" or hearing level, because the initial determination is often cloaked with a presumption of correctness and there is a tendency to defer to the supposed exper-

---

20. Phillips v. San Luis Obispo County Dep't, 228 Cal. Rptr. 101. (Cal. App. 2d 1986)

21. *See also* Pasco v. Reihl, 620 So. 2d 229 (Fla. Dist. Ct. App. 1993), *aff'd*, 635 So. 2d 229 (Fla. 1994) (Statute establishing dangerous dog classification deprived owners of legal property interest without due process and was thus unconstitutional; statute provided no specific guidelines to which classifying agency must conform or specific findings it must articulate in making its final determination classifying dog as dangerous, and statute failed to provide owner of alleged dangerous dog with opportunity to be heard prior to final determination.).

22. 128 P.3d 1241 (Wash. Ct. App. 2006)

tise of the animal control officers even if the hearing is supposed to be *de novo*. As the attorney defending a dog facing destruction or classification as "vicious" or "dangerous," you must be mindful not only to zealously defend the dog at the hearing but also to create an accurate record for appeal. Accordingly, know before you get to the hearing how the proceeding will be memorialized. If the animal control agency does not record the proceeding or have a court reporter present, you should hire a court reporter to ensure that an accurate transcript is available. If the hearing is being recorded and no court reporter is present, you should insist that speakers identify themselves on the record so that an accurate transcript can be prepared.

Cross-Examination of the Animal Control Officer(s)

If the animal control agency has not adopted and published procedural rules that apply to dangerous dog determinations, you should establish this fact through the testimony of the animal control officer or the director of the animal control agency. Further, if the dog that is the subject of the hearing has had no prior encounters with animal control, you should establish the lack of previous violations in the record. Typically the animal control officer was not present during the incident leading to the hearing, and thus his or her efforts to investigate the incident should be explored. Determine who the animal control officer interviewed, especially if the victim was interviewed but not the dog's owner (or handler at the time of the incident). If the dog was impounded, it might be helpful to ask the animal control officer how the dog behaved when the dog was confiscated. For example, "Officer Smith, did you pick up Bowser and take him to the animal shelter?" "How did you transport him?" "Did you use a bite stick or muzzle?" "So you are telling me that the dog that the City wishes to have declared dangerous walked out of the house with a complete stranger and allowed you to pick him up and put him in the truck?"

Direct Testimony of Dog's Owner

If the incident involving the dog was precipitated by an escape, such as the dog getting out through a gate left open or digging out from under a fence, you should elicit testimony about any remedial measures that have been taken to prevent a recurrence, such as buying a lock for the gate or burying wire to prevent digging under the fence. Also, if the dog has been to obedience school or the owner has made a conscientious effort to socialize the dog with people and other animals, those actions should be brought out. If the owner has not taken those steps, you should ask the owner what steps he or she will take to ensure that the dog will not harm someone in the future.

Expert Testimony

It can be very helpful to have the dog evaluated by an experienced animal behaviorist who can assess the presence or absence of aggressive tendencies. The best witnesses typically are either a veterinary behaviorist or an accredited applied animal behaviorist, although an experienced dog trainer may also be effective, especially one who communicates well and has particular knowledge of the breed involved.

If the behavioral evaluation can be videotaped for presentation to the decision maker, the testimony will be far more effective. A behaviorist may also be able to testify as to the inherent differences in aggression towards other animals and aggressiveness towards people, whether or not a dog was provoked in a particular situation, and whether there are veterinary or behavioral factors that might have caused the attack. Veterinarians in general practice typically lack the credentials to render opinions regarding animal behavior, although they may be able to give helpful fact testimony regarding past interactions with the dog.

Conclusion

Courts have consistently upheld dangerous dog statutes as a legitimate exercise of the jurisdiction's police power.[23] However, a vast majority of people who own dogs consider them family members,[24] and the emo-

---

23. David Favre & Peter L. Borchelt, Animal Law and Dog Behavior 197 (Laws. & JJ. Publg. Co., Inc. 1999)

24. Pew Research Ctr., Gauging Family Intimacy: Dogs Edge Cats (Dads Trail Both), http://pewresearch.org/assets/social/pdf/Pets.pdf (Mar. 7, 2006) (noting that 85 percent of dog owners consider their dog to be a member of their family).

tional distress of having a member of one's family arbitrarily removed from a loving home and destroyed cannot be overstated. Further, because dogs are property, overzealous or arbitrary enforcement of a dangerous dog law can and should result in civil liability. Well-written dangerous dog laws require minimum findings before a dog can be subject to stricter regulation, or destruction, and include consideration of provocation or other mitigating circumstances. Further, a dangerous dog law that will survive judicial scrutiny must establish a hearing process that allows owners of allegedly dangerous dogs a full and fair hearing in front of a neutral fact finder pursuant to published procedural guidelines, which include the ability to compel the attendance of witnesses. If the allegedly dangerous dog has been seized, the hearing should be on an expedited basis because prolonged confinement is cruel to both the dog and its human family, or provision made for the dog's release to another suitable location under appropriate restrictions until the decision is final.

Manner of keeping restrictions are intended to protect the public from dogs that have aggressive tendencies, and are not intended to be punitive. Accordingly, registration fines for "dangerous dogs" should reflect the actual increased cost of ensuring compliance, and not be so exorbitant as to be a penalty in disguise.

Finally, regulation of dangerous dogs should be tempered with common sense. A requirement that a "dangerous" dog complete obedience training and be neutered could do far more to protect public safety than strictly confining the dog in isolation such that it becomes more territorial and more aggressive.

Part III

Breed Discrimination
in the Private Sector

Chapter 6

Hounded by Homeowner Associations and Dogged by Zoning Boards: Litigating Breed-Specific Restrictions

DAVID A. FURLOW

Many of the 74 million dogs in the United States (as of 2005) reside within households governed not just by municipal zoning restrictions but also by restrictive covenants, also known as "conditions, covenants, and restrictions," "deed restrictions," and townhome or condominium association rules and restrictions. This chapter examines recent developments and controversies concerning the adoption, interpretation, and enforcement of restrictive covenants by community associations.

The Recent Rise of Community Associations and Restrictive-Covenant Governance

The rise of community associations—including homeowner associations, property-owners' associations, townhome-owners' associations, and condominium-owners associations—and the spread of their restrictive-covenant schemes of governance have made private use restrictions a major part of American life. In 1960, for example, there were only 1,000 or so condominium, planned development, and stock cooperative projects across the country.[1] By 1984, there were over 80,000 of

---

1. *See* Katherine Rosenberry, *Condominium and Homeowner Associations: Should They Be Treated Like "Mini" Governments?*, 8 ZONING & PLANNING L. REP. 153, 153 (Oct. 1985);

these common-interest community associations.[2] Breed-specific limitations are likeliest to occur in restrictive covenants enforced by community associations. The Community Associations Institute, a nonprofit organization that espouses views associated with the management of community associations, estimates that as of 2006, there were 286,000 community associations around the country, that 23.1 million housing units are a part of those community associations, and that 57.0 million Americans live within them.[3] More than 1.7 million Americans serve on community association boards and nearly 200,000 are members of community association committees.

Community associations have grown so much in recent years for a wide variety of reasons. Many believe that they improve or maintain property values. Others prefer the sense of community associated with self-management of a neighborhood. Some associations exist because cash-strapped local municipalities require new developments to take responsibility for many of the services once provided by government— street lighting, garbage pickup, snow removal, road maintenance, and restriction of the animals permitted to live in such neighborhoods.

Community associations range in size from as small as two-unit cooperatives to as large as master-planned communities with upwards of 20,000 units. They are found all over the country. Some of the largest include Columbia, Maryland; Valencia, California; Summerlin, Nevada; Highlands Ranch, Highlands, Colorado; and The Woodlands, Clear Lake City, and First Colony on the outskirts of Houston, Texas. These community associations typically enforce restrictions on animals and every other aspect of their members' lives through restrictive covenants.

Courts have recognized and enforced restrictive covenants that "touch and concern" the land for centuries.[4] In modern America, private restrictive covenants often complement and sometimes take the place of codes, statutory restrictions, and municipal ordinances that

---

Uriel Reichman, *Residential Private Governments: An Introductory Survey,* 43 U. Chi. L. Rev. 253 (1976).

2. Rosenberry, *supra* note 1, Reichman, *supra* note 1.

3. *See* Cmty. Ass'ns Inst., Industry Data, http://www.caionline.org/about/facts.cfm (Nov. 12, 2007).

4. *See, e.g.,* Spencer's Case, 5 Co. Rep. 16a, 77 Eng. Rep. 72 (Q.B. 1583).

restrict the free use of land—especially in the master-planned communities that have sprung up throughout the country in recent years.[5]

The Rise of Breed-Specific and Pet-Specific Restrictive Covenants

Covenants and Ordinances Restricting Livestock and Specific Pets

In recent years, developers, city officials, and interested members of homeowner associations have begun using restrictive covenants to limit the number and type of pets that homeowners, townhome owners, and condominium association members can keep. These restrictions fall into several broad categories:

1. Numerical restrictions, such as "no more than four domestic pets may be kept at any home";
2. Antilivestock restrictions that sometimes lead to disputes over what constitutes "livestock," for example, "The raising or keeping of hogs, horses, poultry, fowls, or other livestock on any part of a subdivision is prohibited . . .";
3. "Conformity" restrictions that limit the acceptable kind of animals to those that conform to a traditional notion of acceptable animals, for example, "No owner shall keep any pet but dogs, cats, birds, or fish in an aquarium"; and
4. Flat "No pets allowed" bans on all kinds of animals.[6]

Breed-Specific Dangerous Dog Restrictions

Concerns about dangers posed by "dangerous" dogs—including 58 fatal dog attacks in the United States in the years 2007 to 2008[7]—as

---

5. *See* Jeffrey A. Goldberg, *Note and Comment: Community Association Use Restrictions: Applying the Business Judgment Doctrine*, 64 Chi.-Kent L. Rev. 653, 653 (1988).

6. *See generally* Note, *Condominium Use Restrictions—The Effect of "No Children, No Pets"*: Covered Bridge Condominium Ass'n v. Chambliss, 38 Baylor L. Rev. 1003 (Fall 1986).

7. NCRC, Types of Dog Bites at http://nationalcanineresearchcouncil.com/dog-bites/types-of-dog-bites/.

well as concerns about the allegedly dangerous proclivities of specific animals and breeds of animals have given rise to new kinds of restrictions that focus on keeping specific animals out of gated communities, condo associations, and deed-restricted communities. A few specific examples of such restrictions can be found in any Internet search.

A number of publications now guide developers, community association officers and directors, and attorneys in drafting pet-prohibitions and breed-specific restrictions. The most prominent among these publications is a 36-page booklet offered on the Community Associations Institute's website: Debra H. Lewin's *Pet Policies: How Community Associations Maintain Peace & Harmony.*[8] Chapter 4, Restrictions and Alternatives, begins with flat "No Pets!" restrictions and then moves on to cover size, breed, and species restrictions.

The adoption, interpretation, enforcement, and appeal of pet- and breed-specific restrictions have unleashed strong emotions and harsh feelings. These restrictive covenants have pitted home-purchasers against sellers and developers, neighbors against neighbors, and homeowners, townhome owners, and condominium residents against their fellow members, officers, directors, attorneys, and insurers. When a recent poll shows that 69 percent of Americans view their pets as members of their families,[9] it is not surprising that these breed-specific disputes are ending up, more and more often, in the courts.

Traditional Rules Governing the Drafting, Interpretation, and Enforcement of Restrictive Covenants

Courts construe restrictive covenants to give the parties the benefit of their bargain under an objective, "contractual," standard. Thus, courts seek to ascertain the objective, not the subjective, intent of the parties.[10] A court must give the restriction the meaning by which the words are

---

8. ISBN 978-9-944715-98-7. The price is $25.00 ($15.00 for CAI members).

9. Harris Poll #120, *Pets Are "Members of the Family" and Two-Thirds of Pet Owners Buy Their Pets Holiday Presents* (Dec. 4, 2007), *available at* http://www.harrisinteractive.com/harris_poll/index.asp?PID=840.

10. Travis Heights Imp. Ass'n v. Small, 662 S.W.2d 406, 409 (Tex. App.-Austin 1983, no writ).

ordinarily understood and interpreted.[11] Because a court must interpret a restriction objectively, it is improper to consider an association officer or committee member's subjective understanding of a given deed restriction or rule.[12] The Texas Supreme Court, a state whose supreme court rulings exemplify the way other courts construe restrictive covenants and deed restrictions, has held that a "purchaser [of real property] is bound by only those restrictive covenants attaching to the property to which he has actual or constructive notice. One who purchases for value and without notice takes the land free of the restriction."[13] The court emphasized that restrictions must be *reasonable,* for only when "restrictions are confined to a lawful purpose and are within reasonable bounds and the language employed is clear, [will] such covenants . . . be enforced."[14]

In *Baker v. Henderson,*[15] the Texas Supreme Court set forth the ground rules regarding enforcement of restrictive covenants:

> Restrictive clauses in instruments concerning real estate must be construed strictly, favoring the grantee and against the grantor, and all doubt should be resolved in favor of the free and unrestricted use of land.
>
> Being in derogation of the fee conveyed by the deed, if there be any ambiguity in the terms of the restrictions, or substantial doubt of its meaning, the ambiguity and doubt should be resolved in favor of the free use of the land.[16]

In general, common law courts hold that restrictions on the use of property must be strictly, not liberally, construed—a doctrine that may have particular application to the enforceability of breed-specific restrictive covenants. In *Wilmoth v. Wilcox,*[17] for example, the Texas Supreme Court ruled that "All doubts must be resolved in favor of the unrestricted use

---

11. Green v. Gerner, 283 S.W. 615, 616 (Tex. Civ. App.-Galveston 1926), *aff'd,* 289 S.W. 999 (Tex. Comm. App. 1927, holding approved); WLR, Inc. v. Borders, 690 S.W.2d 663, 667–668 (Tex. App.-Waco 1985, writ ref'd n.r.e.).

12. *See* Meyerland Cmty. Imp. Ass'n, Inc. v. Temple, 700 S. W .2d 263, 266 (Tex. App.-Houston [1st Dist.] 1985, writ ref'd n.r.e.).

13. Davis v. Huey, 620 S.W.2d 561, 565–66 (Tex. 1981).

14. *Id.* at 565.

15. 137 Tex. 266, 153 S.W.2d 465 (1941).

16. *Id.,* 153 S.W.2d at 471, *cited in* Davis v. Huey, 620 S.W.2d 561, 565 (Tex. 1981) (citations omitted).

17. 734 S.W.2d 656 (Tex. 1987).

of the premises, and the restrictive clause must be construed strictly against the party seeking to enforce it."[18]

In general, courts have construed animal-specific restrictive-covenants and zoning-ordinances strictly, in favor of the free use of land and against absurd results, while resolving doubts in favor of homeowners. One of the earliest and most frequently mentioned "breed-specific restriction" homeowner association cases is *Foster Village Community Association v. Hess.*[19] In *Foster Village Community Association*, the court concluded that a homeowner's decision to keep a pet pig ("Sooey") at home did not violate a residential zoning regulation that prohibited "the keeping of livestock."[20] The association argued that a pig, by definition, is "livestock" while the owner argued that whether the pig is a pet or livestock is determined based upon the "use to which the pig is put."[21] The court scrutinized that restriction in detail, applied the Hawaiian version of the doctrine that courts will not enforce absurd interpretations of restrictions, and held that,

> Under [the community association's] argument, the only animals permitted even as pets in residential areas would be those that are customarily found in a residential neighborhood, such as dogs and cats, or birds . . . Clearly, that would be in derogation of every property owner's right to use his property in any lawful manner.[22]

Affirmative Defenses to Breed-Specific and Pet-Specific Restrictive-Covenant Enforcement Actions

Defendants may have several affirmative defenses to such restrictive covenants, including violation of public policy, statute of limitations, or ambiguity.

---

18. *Id.* at 657. *See also* Woodland Trails N. Cmty. Improvement Ass'n v. Grider, 656 S.W.2d 919, 921 (Tex. App.-Houston [1st Dist.] 1983, *reh'g. denied*, 1983) ("[I]f there should be any doubt as to the meaning of [restrictive covenant's] terms, it must be construed most favorably to the homeowner.").
19. 667 P.2d 850 (Haw. Ct. App. 1983).
20. *Id.* at 852.
21. *Id.* at 853.
22. *Id.* at 855.

Public Policy Issues—Statutory Restrictions

In recent years, the growing debate concerning breed-specific laws has resulted in an increasing number of statewide statutes that limit the power of counties, municipalities, and local authorities to enact legislation that bans or severely restricts owners from keeping specific breeds of dogs. Some of these statutes are specific enough to enable a defendant in a restrictive covenant enforcement action to argue that the state legislature has determined, as a matter of public policy, that breed-specific restrictions are too arbitrary or irrational to be enforced by community associations.

Texas exemplifies those states—which include California, Florida, New York, Oklahoma, Texas, and Virginia, among others—whose legislatures have specifically tied the hands of local governments to enact breed-specific restrictions on dogs. The governing Texas statute reads as follows:

> A county or municipality may place additional requirements or restrictions on dangerous dogs if the requirements or restrictions:
>
> 1. are not specific as to one breed or several breeds of dogs; and
> 2. are more stringent than restrictions provided by this subchapter.[23]

This statue reflects the Texas Legislature's recognition that state law should punish the deed, not the breed.

Similarly, Section 822.041(2) of the Texas Health and Safety Code defines a "dangerous dog" as follows:

> § 822.041(2) "Dangerous dog" means a dog that:
>
> (A) makes an unprovoked attack on a person that causes bodily injury and occurs in a place other than an enclosure in which the dog was being kept and that was reasonably certain to prevent the dog from leaving the enclosure on its own; and
> (B) commits unprovoked acts in a place other than an enclosure in which the dog was being kept and that was reasonably certain to prevent the dog from leaving the enclosure on its

---

23. TEX. HEALTH & SAFETY CODE § 822.047 (Vernon/West 2003) ("Local Regulation of Dangerous Dogs") (emphasis added).

own and those acts cause a person to reasonably believe that
the dog will attack and cause bodily injury to that person.[24]

Thus, in Texas, a defendant alleged to have violated a breed-selective
restrictive-covenant could argue that such a deed restriction violates
public policy as established pursuant to these legislative enactments
that bar local communities from enacting and enforcing breed-selective
ordinances.

Statute of Limitations Defenses

In *Malmgren v. Inverness Forest Civic Club, Inc.*, a panel of the Houston
First Court of Appeals unanimously reversed a summary judgment in
favor of the Inverness Forest Residents Civic Club enforcing a permanent injunction against a long-time resident who offended an officer of
Inverness Forest by keeping a pet Vietnamese pot-bellied pig as barred
by the statute of limitations.[25] This case exemplifies how a homeowner's association can waive any right to bring suit for a deed restriction
violation under the four-year statute of limitations[26] governing alleged
violations of deed restrictions.

In *Malmgren*, the homeowner brought his pig, Whoopi, home to
Inverness Forest during Thanksgiving of 1991. He bought her as a pet,
not as livestock. The summary judgment record contained the affidavit
of a prominent Texas veterinarian who testified that Vietnamese pot-
bellied pigs are sold and purchased solely as exotic pets in Texas. The
First Court of Appeals observed that

> Malmgren testified he brought Whoopi home on Thanksgiving 1991.
> He testified his neighbors have known about Whoopi for years, as he
> showed her to everyone when he first brought her home. He stated
> he has never made any efforts to hide Whoopi from his neighbors or
> Inverness's officers and agents.

---

24. *Id.* § 822.041(2) (Vernon/West 2003)
25. 981 S.W.2d 875 (Tex. App.-Houston [1st Dist.] 1998, no pet. his.).
26. Tex. Civ. Prac. & Rem. Code Ann. § 16.051's four-year statute of limitations governs
suits to enforce deed restrictions. *See* Buzbee v. Castlewood Civic Ctr., 737 S.W.2d 366,
368 (Tex. App.-Houston [14th Dist.] 1987, no writ). Similar two- and four-year statutes
of limitations govern the filing of similar restrictive-covenant enforcement actions around
the country.

Each of Mr. Malmgren's neighbors testified they knew about Whoopi since November 1991, when Malmgren first acquired her. They remembered Malmgren showed Whoopi to everyone. [Malmgren's neighbor Ann] Hammond testified she spoke with Wendell Mosely, an Inverness officer, about Malmgren's keeping Whoopi, when Mosely contacted her to inquire about it. The Colstons [Malmgren's neighbors] and Hammond each testified they never complained about Whoopi.[27]

The association did not file a lawsuit immediately against the homeowner, Malmgren, but waited until the statute of limitations was about to expire to file suit in Harris County Justice of the Peace Court. The association then dismissed its justice court suit after four years and attempted to refile the suit in Harris County District Court.

The First Court of Appeals ruled that the statute of limitations barred Inverness Forest's claim as a matter of law. The First Court of Appeals ruled that limitations began to accrue during Thanksgiving of 1991 when an agent of Inverness Forest, Block Coordinator Wanda Elder, learned that Malmgren was keeping a pet pig:

> Malmgren's summary judgment motion was supported by evidence establishing his [four-year] statute of limitations defense as a matter of law . . . [Wanda] Elder testified she was Inverness's block captain coordinator for many years, including 1991 and 1992. She distinctly remembered watching Whoopi eat watermelon when Malmgren first acquired her in 1991 . . .
>
> [A]s the block captain coordinator she had the power to report violations. Malmgren claims that Inverness is bound by the knowledge of its agent. Malmgren is correct. Under general principles of agency law, notice to an agent is deemed notice to a principal. *See Polland & Cook v. Lehmann*, 832 S.W.2d 729, 738 (Tex. App.–Houston [1st Dist.] 1992, writ denied). Therefore, Elder's knowledge from Thanksgiving 1991 is imputed to Inverness.[28]

Once Malmgren presented that evidence of Inverness Forest agent Wanda Elder's knowledge, "the burden shifted to Inverness to present issues precluding summary judgment."[29] Because Inverness, the

27. 981 S.W.2d at 878.
28. *Id.*
29. *Id.*

homeowner association, failed to present any competent evidence to raise a genuine issue of material fact as to when it first acquired knowledge of Malmgren's keeping of a pot-bellied pig as a pet, the First Court of Appeals ruled that Malmgren had proven his limitations defense as a matter of law.[30]

Contractual Ambiguity as an Affirmative Defense

The affirmative defense of ambiguity might become important to any dog owner facing an enforcement action under an ambiguously written restrictive covenant or zoning ordinance. Is the restriction clear or muddled? Does it apply to specific breeds and, if so, are those breeds clearly and unambiguously defined?

The rules regarding "strict interpretation" versus "liberal interpretation" of deed restrictions, their intent, and purposes come into play when a homeowner and an association go to war over undefined or poorly defined terms and phrases in a set of deed restrictions. A term or phrase can be ambiguous, either as a matter of law or as a matter of fact, if it is subject to two or more differing but reasonable interpretations.[31]

As a preliminary matter, the "ambiguity" of a contract is a matter of law for a court to decide by looking at the contract as a whole in light of the circumstances present when the contract was signed.[32] If a court concludes that a contract is ambiguous, a court may properly admit extraneous evidence of the parties' intent when one drafted or both negotiated the disputed contractual language.[33] A jury, then, is entitled to decide the meaning of ambiguous language under Texas Pattern Jury Charge 101.8, which includes the instruction:

---

30. *Id.* at 879. David A. Weatherbie tersely summarized the result of the *Malmgren* case:

> In 1995, the owners association brought a lawsuit to remove Whoopi from the neighborhood. They failed. It had been more than four years since the association discovered, via the block captain, that Whoopi was there, and the statute of limitations had run.

D.A. Weatherbie, *Real Property*, 52 SMU L. Rev. 1393, 1497 (Summer 1999).
31. Nat'l Union Fire Ins. Co. v. CBI Indus., Inc., 907 S.W.2d 517, 520 (Tex. 1995).
32. *Id; see also* R & P Enters. v. LaGuarta, Gavrel & Kirk, Inc., 596 S.W.2d 517, 518 (Tex. 1980).
33. *Nat'l Union,* 907 S.W.2d at 520; *R & P Enters.,* 596 S.W.2d at 518.

It is your duty to interpret the following language of the agreement: [Insert ambiguous language]. You must decide its meaning by determining the intent of the parties at the time of the agreement. Consider all of the facts and circumstances surrounding the making of the agreement, the interpretation placed on the agreement by the parties, and the conduct of the parties.

A homeowner should ask a trial court to instruct a jury that all doubts must be resolved in favor of the free and unrestricted use of the premises, and the restrictive clause must be construed strictly against the party seeking to enforce it.[34]

Some of the most useful "ambiguity" case law has arisen in restrictive covenant cases involving undefined terms such as "structure" or "building." For example, in *Turner v. England*,[35] a Texas court studied the issue of whether a flat concrete pad serving as a tennis court constituted a "structure" within the meaning of the deed restrictions.[36] This is how the Eastland Court of Appeals analyzed the issue of what constitutes a "structure":

The property owners, Malcolm and Jo Ann Turner, began construction of a $40,000 tennis court on their lot. The neighbors, Richard W. England and others, secured a permanent injunction which commanded the owners "to cease and desist and refrain from constructing a tennis court . . . in any manner that does not comply with paragraph 10 of the restrictive covenants [that prohibited constructing a 'building, fence or other structure']." The property owners appeal the judgment which was rendered on January 20, 1981, following a nonjury trial. *We reverse the judgment, dissolve the injunction, and render judgment that plaintiff and intervenors take nothing.*[37]

The *Turner* court held, "It is well settled in Texas that 'restrictive covenants are to be strictly construed against those who seek to restrict the

---

34. Pebble Beach Prop. Owners' Ass'n v. Sherer, 2 S.W.3d 283 (Tex. App.-San Antonio 1999, writ denied) (citing *Wilmouth* after first citing *Pilarcik*); Simon Group v. May Dep't Stores, 943 S.W.2d 64, 71 (Tex. App.-Corpus Christi 1997, no writ); *see also* Munson v. Milton, 948 S.W.2d 813, 816 (Tex. App.-San Antonio 1997, writ denied) ("If there is any ambiguity or doubt as to the intent, the covenant is to be strictly construed against the party seeking to enforce it in favor of the free and unrestricted use of land.").
35. 628 S.W.2d 213 (Tex. App.-Eastland 1982, writ ref'd n.r.e.).
36. *Id.* at 214–16.
37. *Id.* at 214 (emphasis added).

use of property and that all doubt must be resolved in favor of the free use of the property."[38] The court further emphasized that the concrete slab was "level with the ground and that there is no plan to place any item above ground elevation within 50 feet of the street. The poles for the net will be further than 50 feet from the street, as will the lighting fixtures."[39] To constitute a "building" under Texas law, a structure had to be enclosed.[40] Thus, a flat, concrete tennis court or similar slab would not constitute either a "structure" or a "building" under that and similar case law.

In fact, this is generally what courts have ruled in cases involving restrictions that do a poor job of defining "structure," "building," or "construction." For example, a Louisiana court ruled that concrete slabs for air conditioners did not constitute buildings, garages, or outbuildings in the context of deed restrictions[41] while a New York court ruled that another flat concrete surface, a highway, did not constitute a "building"[42] in a restrictive covenant case. Similarly, in other restrictive covenant cases, a West Virginia court ruled that a railroad spur did not constitute a "building,"[43] while the Georgia Supreme Court[44] held that the word "building" does not include every erection on land, such as fences, gates, or other structures. The Georgia Court concluded that the term "building" referred only to residential structures.

In summation, legal analysis and a dogged defense can save a cherished pet.

---

38. *Id.* (citing Davis v. Huey, 620 S.W.2d 561 (Tex.1981)); Southampton Civic Club v. Couch, 159 Tex. 464, 322 S.W.2d 516 (Tex. 1958)).

39. *Id.* at 215–16.

40. Waddell v. State, 918 S.W.2d 91, 94 n.3 (Tex. App.-Dallas 1990, no pet. his.); Day v. State, 534 S.W.2d 681, 684–85 (Tex. Crim. App. 1976).

41. Metry Club Gardens Ass'n v. Newman, 182 So. 2d 712 (La. Ct. App. 1966).

42. Mairs v. Stevens, 268 A.D. 922, 51 N.Y.S.2d 286 (N.Y. Sup. Ct., App. Div. 1944), *aff'd*, 294 N.Y. 806, 294 N.Y.S. 806 (1945).

43. Neekamp v. Huntington Chamber of Commerce, 99 W. Va. 388, 129 S.E. 314 (W. Va. Sup. Ct. App. 1925).

44. Randall v. Atlanta Advertising Serv., 159 Ga. 217, 125 S.E. 462 (1924).

Chapter 7

Homeowners Insurance and Dog Ownership: A Primer

LARRY CUNNINGHAM

Introduction

Many homeowners insurance companies engage in a practice known as "breed discrimination."[1] They will systematically deny coverage, or refuse to renew existing policies, to a homeowner who has a dog belonging to one of several breeds that the insurance industry considers to be inherently dangerous.[2] Such coverage decisions are decided

---

1. *See generally* Larry Cunningham, *The Case Against Dog Breed Discrimination by Homeowner's Insurance Company*, 11 CONN. INS. L.J. 1 (2004), available at http://www.animallaw.info/articles/aruscunningham2005.htm and http://papers.ssrn.com/sol3/papers.cfm?abstract_id=711182.

2. *Id.* at 11–13 (documenting media reports about breed discrimination) and 13–16 (insurance industry defense of breed discrimination); John Reynolds, *One woman's lovable pet might be an insurance company's nightmare*, SPRINGFIELD STATE JOURNAL-REGISTER, Feb. 5, 2008, at 1; Doug Finke, *Some insurers are wary of certain breeds of dog*, SPRINGFIELD STATE JOURNAL-REGISTER, Jan. 29, 2008, at 2; Dee Carlson, *Your Pit Bull Could Up Insurance Rates*, SEATTLE POST-INTELLIGENCER, Nov. 16, 2007, at B7; Jeff Bertolucci, *Man's Best Friend but Insurers' Foe: Their Assembly Bill Has Failed, but Dog Lovers Continue to Rail Against Breed Discrimination*, L.A. TIMES, June 6, 2004, at K1; Vincent J. Schodolski, *"Bad" Dogs Put Costly Bite on Insurers, Homeowners*, CHI. TRIB., May 17, 2004, at 1; Jeff Bertolucci, *Is Nothing Private? Home Insurers Ask About Everything from Rover to Rolexes. And the Answers Matter*, L.A. TIMES, May 9, 2004, at K1; Allan Woods, *Rottweilers, Pit Bulls New Insurance Liability*, NAT'L POST, Mar. 26, 2004, at A3; Michele Derus, *Dog Bites Giving Insurers Pause*, MILWAUKEE J. & SENTINEL, Feb. 29, 2004, at 1F; Gloria Campisi, *Beware of Dog When Seeking Insurance; Some Firms Have "Bad Breed" Lists*, PHILA. DAILY NEWS, Oct. 7, 2003, at 14; Ryan Slight, *Liability Factor Can Hurt Homeowners*, SPRINGFIELD NEWS LEADER (Mo.), Sept. 28, 2003, at 6A; William Sweet, *Insurers in Doghouse with Some Pet Owners*, SPRINGFIELD UNION-NEWS (MASS.), Aug. 19, 2003, at A1; Purva Patel, *A Bite to the Pocket, Home Insurers Often Charge Higher Premiums Because of Dogs*, SUN-SENTINEL (FT. LAUDERDALE, FLA.), Aug. 12, 2003, at 1D; Charles Toutant, *Insurers Attempt to Leash Dog-Bite Claims: Small-Scale Nuisance Litigation Turning into Big Business*, 29 CONN. L. TRIB. 8 (Aug. 11, 2003); Jim Spencer, *Homeowners Insurance Rules Not For the Dogs*, DAILY PRESS (VA.), Jan. 10, 2003 at C1.

without regard to the individual characteristics of the homeowner's dog. Rather than considering a dog's bite history or other incidences of aggression, an insurance company will consider the dog's breed to be too dangerous to take the risk of coverage.[3]

This chapter explores, from scientific, legal, and policy standpoints, the practice of breed discrimination. Breed discrimination is not supported by the scientific studies on dog bites and thus, without an actuarial justification for this practice, is legally unsound. From a policy standpoint, the lack of scientific basis for the practice, combined with the detrimental effects on individuals and society that result from breed discrimination, should result in a legislative or administrative ban.

Breed Discrimination: Practice and Purported Justifications

Breed discrimination has its origins in breed-specific legislation (BSL), which was enacted in several states and municipalities in the 1980s and 1990s in response to a series of fatal dog bites.[4] BSL regulated, or in some cases outright banned, the ownership of certain breeds of dog.[5] BSL and breed discrimination share a common premise that certain breeds are inherently dangerous. Breeds that are subject of both BSL and blanket insurance treatment include pit bulls, Rottweilers, presa Canarios, chow chows, and German shepherds.[6] Court challenges to BSL by dog owners and animal groups have been largely unsuccessful.[7]

---

3. Ins. Info. Inst., *Dog Bite Liability*, http://www.iii.org/media/hottopics/insurance/dogbite/.

4. Karyn Grey, Note, *Breed-Specific Legislation Revisited: Canine Racism or the Answer to Florida's Dog Control Problems?*, 27 Nova. L. Rev. 415, 417 (2003); Julie A. Thorne, Note, *If Spot Bites the Neighbor, Should Dick and Jane Go to Jail?*, 39 Syracuse L. Rev. 1445 (1988).

5. *Id.*

6. Stephanie Davis, *ASPCA/HSUS campaign tackles insurance industry*, 34:11 DVM 1, 1 (Nov. 2003).

7. *See generally* Russell G. Donaldson, Annotation, *Validity and Construction of Statute, Ordinance or Regulation Applying to Specific Dog Breeds, Such as "Pit Bulls" or "Bull Terriers"*, 80 A.L.R.4th 70 (2004); Lynn Marmer, *The New Breed of Municipal Dog Control Laws: Are They Constitutional?*, 53 U. Cin. L. Rev. 1067 (1984); Heather K. Pratt, Comment, *Canine Profiling: Does Breed-Specific Legislation Take a Bite Out of Canine Crime?*, 108 Penn. St. L. Rev. 855 (2004).

Beginning in 2003 and 2004, news reports began to emerge about insurance companies refusing to provide property insurance to people who owned certain breeds of dog.[8] Certain stories were laughable. The Cranaans of San Antonio, Texas, lost their homeowners insurance because of Bukarus, their 12-year-old Rottweiler. Bukarus, however, was hardly a threat to anyone. He was deaf, partially blind, and had arthritis.[9]

As a result of a perceived increase in people losing, or not being able to obtain, insurance, the Humane Society of the United States and other organizations began tracking breed discrimination. One of the concerns among the animal welfare community was that the practice was leading to increased shelter drop-offs: Families, when forced to choose between their homes or their pets, chose their homes and abandoned their dogs at already overcrowded shelters.[10]

Meanwhile, the insurance industry began to respond to criticisms of the practice. They asserted that certain breeds were too dangerous to insure and cited various studies from the Centers for Disease Control (CDC).[11] That is, certain breeds were more likely to bite people or others' pets. They explained that as businesses, they had to limit their risks, and owners with certain breeds posed unacceptably high risks for liability claims. In support, the Insurance Information Institute (III), a trade group, pointed out that the industry was paying large sums of money for dog bite liability claim. In 2007, it was $356.2 million.[12]

Some perspective is in order, however, regarding this seemingly large amount of money. Claims paid out as a result of dog bites represent a very small percentage of an average insurance company's claims budget. In 2006, property damage ($47 paid out per $100 in premiums collected) far exceeded even all liability claims combined ($3 per $100). Indeed, damage due to lightning, fire, and mold all individually account

---

8. *See* articles listed, *supra* note 2.

9. Patrick McMahon, *Dog owners' new policy: Bite back*, USA Today, May 20, 2003, at 03a.

10. Brian Sodergren, *Insurance Companies Unfairly Target Specific Dog Breeds*, http://www.hsus.org/pets/issues_affecting_our_pets/insurance_companies_unfairly_target_specific_dog_breeds.html.

11. *Dog Bite Liability, supra* note 3.

12. *Id.*

for more claims payouts than all liability claims combined.[13] Dog-bite claims themselves account for approximately one-quarter of liability claims. In sum, they make up $10.75 for every $100 in premiums—a negligible amount.[14]

The Scientific Evidence

Contrary to the III's position, the scientific evidence does not support the conclusion that certain breeds are inherently more dangerous than others.

In order to compare one breed to another, a researcher would have to discover, accurately, two numbers: first, the number of bites per breed, and, second, the number of dogs in a particular breed. Only then could accurate ratios of bites per breed be calculated.[15] There are two major problems, however. First, it is very difficult, if not impossible, to get an accurate count of the number of dog bites.[16] For a variety of reasons, the CDC is unable to track the number of *fatal* dog bites each year.[17] There are even greater difficulties with tabulating nonfatal attacks.[18] There is no national registry of dog bites[19] and, in fact, many dog bites go unreported.[20] Moreover, victims of dog attacks are frequently unable to identify correctly the breed of the dog that bit them.[21] They often

13. Ins. Info. Inst., *Homeowners Insurance*, http://www.iii.org/media/facts/statsbyissue/homeowners/.

14. Cunningham, *supra* note 1, at 15.

15. Jeffrey J. Sacks, Leslie Sinclair, Julie Gilchrist, Gail C. Golab, & Randall Lockwood, *Breeds of dogs involved in fatal human attacks in the United States between 1979 and 1998*, 217 J. Am. Veterinary Med. Ass'n 836, 838 (Sep. 15, 2000).

16. Harold B. Weiss, Deborah L. Friedman, & Jeffrey H. Coben, *Incidence of Dog Bite Injuries Treated in Emergency Departments*, 279 JAMA 51, 51 (1998).

17. Sacks, et al., *supra* note 15, at 838.

18. See generally Cunningham, *supra* note 1, at Part II.A.2.

19. Weiss, et al., *supra* note 16, at 51.

20. Yue-Fang Chang, Joan E. McMahon, Deidre L. Hennon, Ronald E. LaPorte, & Jeffrey H. Coben, *Dog Bite Incidence in the City of Pittsburgh: A Capture-Recapture Approach*, 87:10 Am. J. Pub. Health 1703, 1704 (Oct. 1997).

21. American Veterinary Medical Association, Task Force on Canine Aggression and Human-Canine Interactions, *A community approach to dog bite prevention*, 218 J. Am. Veterinary Med. Ass'n 1732, 1733 (2001) [hereinafter Task Force]; Kenneth A. Gershman, Jeffrey J. Sacks, and John C. Wright, *Which Dogs Bite? A Case-Control Study of Risk Factors*, 93 Pediatrics 913, 916 (1994); John C. Wright, *Canine Aggression Toward People: Bite Scenarios and Prevention*, 21:2 Veterinary Clinics of North America: Small Animal Practice 299, 301 (1991).

assume that anything with pointed ears and blue eyes is a "husky;" a muscular, midsize dog is a "pit bull;" a dog that is fluffy is a chow chow; and if it has black and tan marks it must be a Rottweiler. The problem of misidentification is compounded by the prevalence of mixed-breed "mutts"[22] and the fact that certain "breeds" are not really breeds at all. "Pit bull," for example refers to a class of three separate breeds: American Staffordshire Terrier, Staffordshire Pit Bull Terrier, and Bull Terrier.[23] Finally, it is doubtful that "just cause" bites—situations in which the dog was justified in biting, such as to defend itself or its owner from an attacker—should be included in the number.[24] Yet no mechanism exists to screen out such cases from the calculations.

The second major problem is that there is no "dog census."[25] Without an accurate count of the number of each breed, it is impossible to compare breeds to one another. For example, if two breeds each had 100 bites during a given year, but Breed A had twice as many members as Breed B, then Breed B would be twice as dangerous as Breed A. There is, however, no accurate count of the number of dogs per breed. Registries, such as the American Kennel Club's, rely on voluntary reporting by dog owners and greatly undercount any given breed.[26] Mixed breeds and homeless dogs present additional challenges to obtaining an accurate population count for each breed.[27]

It is for these reasons that CDC scientists and other researchers have concluded that dog-bite statistics are incomplete and should not be used by legislatures, insurance companies, or other decision-makers to make categorical judgments about particular breeds of dog.[28]

22. Sacks, et al., *supra* note 15, at 838.
23. American Dog Owners Assoc., Inc. v. City of Lynn, 533 N.E.2d 642, 644 (Mass. 1989).
24. Cunningham, *supra* note 1, at 34–35.
25. Randall Lockwood & Kate Rindy, *Are "Pit Bulls" Different? An Analysis of the Pit Bull Terrier Controversy*, 1:1 Anthrozoös 2, 2–3 (1987).
26. Mark Derr, *The Politics of Dogs*, THE ATLANTIC MONTHLY, Mar., 1990, at 49, 50.
27. Sacks, et al., *supra* note 15; Derr, *supra* note 26.
28. *See, e.g.*, Jeffrey J. Sacks, Randall Lockwood, Janet Hornreich, & Richard W. Sattin, *Fatal Dog Attacks*, 1989-1994, 97:6 PEDIATRICS 891, 894 (June 1996).

The Values of Pets and Homeownership

The counterbalancing values of dog ownership and homeownership, particularly when combined with the lack of scientific evidence to support BSL or breed discrimination, make a compelling case against such practices. Pet ownership is at an all-time high in this country. Billions of dollars are spent annually on veterinary care, food, "pet vacation resorts," and cemeteries.[29] Money aside, most pet owners regard their dogs, cats, and other animals as members of their families.[30] Such devotion is sometimes taken to what some would call an extreme degree. For example, many physicians can recount at least one patient who refused hospitalization because no one would be available to care for a pet.[31]

Breed discrimination makes it difficult, if not impossible, for a segment of the population to obtain a home. Most people cannot afford to buy a house without taking out a mortgage. In turn, lending institutions will not give a person a mortgage without proof that the property securing the mortgage is insured against property damage and liability claims. Homeowners insurance is therefore the gatekeeper to homeownership.[32] No insurance, no mortgage; no mortgage, no house. This has significant negative consequences for both individuals and society at large. By purchasing a residence, a person builds equity that can be used for retirement or as a means of passing wealth down through generations.[33] Furthermore, a homeowner is more likely to care about his or her community. Breed discrimination forces a dog owner to make a painful choice: give up a beloved pet, move to a rental property, or commit insurance fraud by lying about the dog's existence.

---

29. Richard Willing, *Under Law, Pets Are Becoming Almost Human*, USA TODAY, Sept. 13, 2000, at 1A.
30. Task Force, *supra* note 21, at 1739.
31. *Id.* at 1740.
32. NAACP v. American Family Mutual Ins. Co., 978 F.2d 287, 297 (7th Cir. 1992).
33. David H. Harris, Jr., *Using the Law to Break Discriminatory Barriers to Fair Lending for Home Ownership*, 22 N.C. CENT. L.J. 101, 101 (1996).

A Legal and Policy Response
to Breed Discrimination

Because of its quasi-public nature, the insurance industry is highly regulated by, and serves at the pleasure of, state governments. A state may regulate everything about insurance—from advertising to trade practices to the very setting of prices.[34] Some states require insurers to write policies for particular risks, even though the marketplace may have determined such insureds to be poor risks. In other words, even when an insurance company can show an "actuarial justification" for a particular risk—that is, a sufficient link between a certain risk factor and actual claims—a state may prohibit the use of that risk factor in underwriting decisions, due to countervailing societal interests.[35] For example, in the mid-1990s, there was documented evidence that insurance companies were denying health, life, and disability coverage to victims of domestic violence because statistical evidence showed that such persons had higher risks for claims. Critics of this practice called for regulation, notwithstanding the statistical or "actuarial justification" for the insurer's decisions. Many states responded with laws prohibiting the denial of insurance coverage based on an insured's status as a victim of domestic violence.[36] Breed discrimination is different because insurers do not even have a scientific basis for their hunch that certain breeds of dog are more dangerous than others. However, even if such a basis existed, they then would have to overcome the hurdle of showing that the social costs of denying coverage were warranted.

The concept of actuarial justification is rooted in the laws or regulations of every state.[37] Actuarially justified underwriting is not only

---

34. Blue Cross & Blue Shield of Central New York, Inc. v. McCall, 674 N.E.2d 1124, 1126 (N.Y. 1996); Bekken v. Equitable Life Assurance Soc'y, 293 N.W. 200, 211 (N.D. 1940); 43 Am. Jur. 2d *Insurance* § 23 (2004).

35. *See, e.g.,* Elizabeth C. Price, *The Evolution of Health Care Decision-Making: The Political Paradigm and Beyond,* 65 Tenn. L. Rev. 619, 626 (1998) (discussing regulation of insurance practice of requiring discharge of new mothers within hours of giving birth).

36. See Deborah S. Hellman, *Is Actuarially Fair Insurance Pricing Actually Fair?: A Case Study in Insuring Battered Women,* 32 Harv. C.R.-C.L. L. Rev. 355 (1997).

37. Sonia M. Suter, *Disentangling Privacy From Property: Toward a Deeper Understanding of Genetic Privacy,* 72 Geo. Wash. L. Rev. 737 (2004) ("All states require underwriting decisions to be actuarially, or rationally, based; they cannot be arbitrary. Insurers must engage in good-faith practices in deciding whether to underwrite, at what rate, and for what conditions."); 43 Am. Jur. 2d *Insurance* § 43 (2003) (underwriting and rate setting may take into account only legitimate cost factors).

the law, it is good business. By *accurately* separating out risks into "not insurable" and "insurable" (and, then, in turn, separating out insurable risks into various risk classifications), actuarially justified underwriting promotes efficiency and profit.[38] Consumers are not allowed into the insurance pool when the likelihood of loss is so high that inclusion of their risks threatens the viability of the pool itself.[39] For those insureds allowed in the pool, actuarially justified underwriting promotes efficiency by assigning low premiums to low-risk insureds and high premiums to insureds more likely to have a claim. This creates a market incentive for low-risk insureds to participate in the pool as opposed to self-selecting out of insurance.[40] Accurate risk classification also maximizes profits for the insurer. By eliminating the highest-risk insureds from the pool, an insurer keeps premiums low for the low-risk insureds who remain.[41] An insurer who does not maintain its "classification edge" faces the potential of having its low-risk insureds leave to join other companies who are able to charge lower premiums due to better risk classification decisions.[42] The insurer is stuck with its high-risk insureds as well as the high-risk insureds who migrate over from the insurer's competition. This means that the insurer is not maximizing its profitability.[43]

The fact is that because an adequate scientific basis does not exist for breed discrimination, insurance companies are making inaccurate risk classifications. They are excluding from the insurance pool many people who would otherwise be good, low-risk customers. This overly cautious approach to underwriting comes with great social cost: the loss of either a valued pet or the opportunity to purchase a home.

---

38. Tom Baker, *Containing the Promise of Insurance: Adverse Selection and Risk Classification*, 9 CONN. INS. L.J. 371, 377 (2002/2003).

39. *Id.*

40. *Id.* at 373.

41. *Id.*

42. KENNETH S. ABRAHAM, DISTRIBUTING RISK: INSURANCE, LEGAL THEORY, AND PUBLIC POLICY 67–68 (1986).

43. Baker, *supra* note 38, at 378.

Conclusion

Unless and until the insurance industry presents evidence demonstrating a sound, scientific link between certain breeds and dangerousness, the practice of breed discrimination should be administratively or legislatively banned as a violation of the principle of actuarially justified underwriting. Even if the industry can bring forth evidence to support breed discrimination, legislators and regulators should give careful consideration to the countervailing benefits of pet and home ownership and the social costs associated with denial of those benefits.

Index

Page numbers followed by the letter "n" indicate references to footnotes.

A

Actuarial justification, 93–94
Aggression, causes of, 18
Ambiguity, contractual, 84–86
American Kennel Club, 13
American Pet Products
    Association, 8
American Temperament Test
    Society (ATTS), 10
Animal control officer
    balance in job of, 61
    cross-examination of, 69
    discretion of, 62–63
    as witness, 42–43
Animals, as victims, 40–41
Anna Cieslwicz Act, 22
Attacks
    animals as victims of, 40–41
    children as victims of, 9–10
    rarity of, 1

B

Baker v. Henderson, 79
Bans, on pit bulls, 7
Best Friends Animal Sanctuary, 2
BioPet Vet Lab, 11
Bradley, Janis, 8
Breed discrimination
    DNA testing and, 11–15
    insurance and, 89–90
    justifications for, 88–90
    legal and policy response to,
        93–94

origin of, 9
    practice of, 88–90
    scientific evidence for, 90–91
Breed identification
    DNA testing and, 14–15
    in legislation, 26
    problems with, 13
    in *Toledo v. Tellings*, 29
Breed-specific legislation. *See also*
        Toledo v. Tellings
    breed definition in, 26
    challenges to, 34–36
    as civil or criminal, 27
    constitutional challenges
        to, 26
    equal protection and, 35
    penalties in, 27
    privileges and immunities
        challenges to, 35–36
    procedural due process and,
        34–35
    restrictions on, 81–82
    substantive due process
        and, 35
    vagueness of, 34
Breed-specific restrictive
        covenants, 77–78
Brentano Math and Science
        Academy, 23

C

Calgary, 20
Care, aggression and, 18
Carter v. City of Stuart, 61n
Cases, classes of, 39–40
Cats, attacks on, 40–41
Centers for Disease Control, 89

Chaining, 21, 40
Chain of custody, 45
Children, as victims, 9–10
Cieslewicz, Anna, 22
Commerce clauses, 33–34
Community associations, rise of,
    75–77
Community Associations
    Institute, 76
Community-policing approach,
    20–21
Contractual ambiguity, as
    affirmative defense,
    84–86
Culpability, of owners, 39–41

D
Dangerous Dog Act (Spain),
    15–16
Dangerous Dog Act (United
    Kingdom), 15
Dangerous Dog Law (Virginia),
    47–59
Defense, of dog at hearing,
    68–70
Delise, Karen, 11, 17
Denver, CO, 16–17
Discretion, of animal control
    officers, 62–63
Discrimination
    DNA testing and, 11–15
    insurance and, 89–90
    justifications for, 88–90
    legal and policy response to,
        93–94
    origin of, 9
    practice of, 88–90
    scientific evidence for, 90–91

DNA evidence collection, 42
DNA expert, 45
DNA sampling, 22
DNA testing, 11–15
Due process, 26, 30–33, 34–35,
    63–68

E
Elder, Wanda, 83
Equal protection, 31–33, 35
Evidence, 42
Expert testimony, 70

F
Fatal attacks, incidence of, 1
Forensic nurses, 43–44
*Foster Village Community
    Association v. Hess*, 80
Fundamental due process, 26

G
George Washington University
    Law School, 2
Gratuitous hearings,
    67–68
Guard dogs, 1

H
Henshall, Charles, 63–66
High-risk owners, 18–20
Home owners' associations. *See*
    community associations
Homeownership values, 92
House Resolution 1026
    (Illinois), 23
Humane Care for Animals
    Act, 19

I

Illinois, 19
Illinois Animal Control
    Act, 22
Injury, severe, 65n
Insurance, 89–90

J

*Journal of Animal and Veterinary
    Advances,* 18
Journal of Injury Prevention,
    9–10
*Journal of the American Veterinary
    Medical Association,* 9
Judicial review, 28–29
Justifications, for breed
    discrimination, 88–90

K

Knox County, Tennessee, 22

L

Laws
    in Alberta, 20
    community-policing
        approach, 20–21
    in Denver, 16–17
    DNA testing and, 14–15
    effectiveness of, 15–18
    failure of, 1–2
    in Illinois, 19
    in Minnesota, 19, 20
    problems with, 2
    restricting ownership,
        18–20
    restricting tethering, 21
    in Spain, 15–16

in Texas, 81–82
in UK, 15
in Virginia, 41, 47–59
in Washington, 19
Livestock, 77, 80

M

*Malmgren v. Inverness Forest Civic
    Club, Inc.,* 82–84
Mansour v. King County, 68
MMI Genomics, 11

N

National Canine Research
    Council, 11
Neighbors, as witnesses, 43
Nurses, forensic, 43–44

O

Owners
    aggression and, 18
    culpability of, 39–41
    high-risk, 18–20
    testimony of, 69–70

P

Packs, of dogs, 22, 40
Pasco v. Reihl, 68n
Pet ownership values, 92
Physicians, treating, 44
Pit bulls
    bans on, 7
    breeds considered, 8
    temperament of, 10–12
    in *Toledo v. Tellings,*
        28–29
Police officer, 42–43

Population
  increase in, 8
  of U.S. dogs, 1
Port St. Lucie, FL, 62–63, 66–68
Privileges and immunities,
    33–34, 35–36
Procedural due process, 30–31,
    34–35, 66–68
Prosecution witnesses, 41–46

R
Restrictive covenants
  affirmative defenses to, 80–86
  breed- and pet-specific, 77–78
  rise of, 75–77
  rules governing drafting of,
    78–80
Rose v. Salem, 62

S
St. John's University School of
    Law, 3
St. Paul, MN, 19
Sentell v. New Orleans, 62
Severe injury, 65n
Spain, 15–16
State veterinarian, 44
Statute of limitations defenses,
    82–84
Substantive due process, 31–33,
    35, 63–66
Sullivan, Dorothy, 41

T
Tacoma, WA, 19
Takings, 33–34, 35–36
Temperament, 10–12
Tethering, 21, 40
Texas, 81–82

Toledo v. Tellings
  appeal in, 29
  background of, 27–28
  equal protection in, 31–33
  judicial review of, 28–29
  in Ohio Supreme Court, 30
  overview of, 25
  privileges and immunities in,
    33–34
  procedural due process in,
    30–31
  substantive due process in,
    31–33
  takings argument in, 33–34
Treating physicians, 44
Turner v. England, 85–86
Twain, Mark, 7

U
United Kennel Club, 13
United Kingdom, 15
United States Code Section
    1983, 14, 14n

V
Vagueness, 34
Values, 92
Veterinarians, as witnesses, 44
Viciousness, definition of, 29
Victim, as witness, 41–42
Virginia, 41, 47–59
Volusia County Animal Board,
    64–66

W
Wilmoth v. Wilcox, 79–80
Witnesses, for prosecution,
    41–46
Woodward, Jim, 24n